The Student Enneagram: The Secret
to Leveling-Up Our Kids at Home & in the Classroom

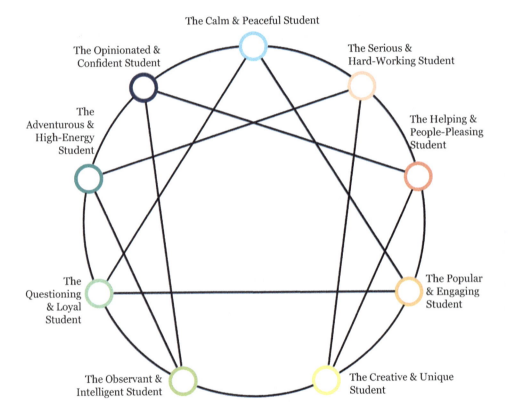

The *Student* Enneagram

The Secret to Leveling-Up Our Kids at Home & in the Classroom

The Student Enneagram: The Secret to
Leveling-Up Our Kids at Home & in the Classroom

Copyright © 2022 Sarah Waxman

All rights reserved. This book is protected by the copyright laws of the
United States of America. No part of this book may be reproduced or used
in any manner without the prior written permission of the copyright
owner.

Limit of Liability/Disclaimer of Warranty: The advice and strategies
contained herein may not be suitable for every situation. This work is sold
with the understanding that the author is not engaging in rendering
medical, legal, or other professional advice or services. If professional
assistance is required, the services of a medical or mental health
professional should be sought. The author shall not be liable for damages
arising herein. Readers should be aware that websites listed in this book
may have changed or disappeared since publish date.

Paperback ISBN: 979-8-9864714-1-9
Hardback ISBN: 979-8-9864714-0-2
eBook ISBN: 979-8-9864714-2-6

Edited by: Ashley D Inc.
Cover Design by: Elizabeth Levrets-Ortiz
Cover Photo by: Sarah Waxman
Back Cover Photo by: Ria B Photography
Script Fonts: KA Designs
Layout by: Sarah Waxman
Photo on Page 12: halayalex. www.freepik.com

Printed in the United States of America

Dedicated To:

Mike, my wonderful and incredibly supportive husband. I wouldn't be doing what I am doing without you or your encouragement of me chasing my dreams and doing the things.

Daniel and Sullivan, my two sweet and incredible boys. Nothing means more to me than being your mom. Thank you for inspiring me and challenging me to be a better mom each day. Thank you for always staying true to who you are and for lighting up the world with your personalities.

Teachers, administrators, and parents who believe that self-awareness and personal growth are important elements of education.

"Each of us perceives the world from a unique perspective. While each perspective is valid, it is limited. Our personality shapes the way we interact with the world: how we teach, learn, work, and communicate. As teachers, our personality type makes us more comfortable with certain teaching styles over others. As students, our personality type makes us prefer certain ways of learning.

As a teacher, you interact with many students, most of whom probably see the world differently than you do. Different perspectives, values, and preferences sometimes lead to misunderstanding and frustration.

Each of the nine Enneagram types has a different motivation. Our motivation is a powerful force that drives most of our behavior. When the world around us supports and reinforces our motivation, a strong tailwind aligns with all our energy, propelling us strongly toward our aspirations. Find ways to align with your students' motivation and watch them soar."

Rob Fitzel

"The Enneagram is an amazing tool to help people grow in self-awareness, and in their relationships, too! With insight and an encouraging approach, Sarah Waxman guides educators, administrators, and parents to be able to gain a little bit of insight from the behaviors, patterns, and tendencies that students are demonstrating. You will be blessed for reading it."

Beth McCord, *Your Enneagram Coach*

"Sarah is the go-to expert when it comes to using the Enneagram in the classroom. The Student Enneagram allows educators, administrators, and parents to view each child holistically and learn the parts of an individual that we don't always see from the outside. You will learn so much by reading this book!"

Ashton Whitmoyer-Ober, *Creator of @enneagramashton*

Table of Contents

Introduction: .... page 9
The Student Enneagram: .... page 12
The Type 1 Student: .... page 26
The Type 2 Student: .... page 42
The Type 3 Student: .... page 56
The Type 4 Student: .... page 72
The Type 5 Student: .... page 88
The Type 6 Student: .... page 104
The Type 7 Student: .... page 122
The Type 8 Student: .... page 138
The Type 9 Student: .... page 156
Putting It All Together: .... page 172
Acknowledgements: .... page 177
About The Author: .... page 179
References: .... page 180

Introduction

Wow. First of all, thank you for choosing this book. I'm truly humbled. Teachers, administrators, and parents, this is for you. Your jobs are far from easy. I'm Sarah Dutton Waxman, a certified Enneagram coach and former educator. I taught middle school for nearly 11 years. Most of those years were spent in a regular classroom, but the last year was in a virtual classroom, thanks to COVID-19 and the 2020 pandemic.

I began working on this book during the winter of my ninth year. I was first introduced to the Enneagram in 2019 and found it to be incredibly fascinating. Initially, I only used the information for myself. However, during the 2019-2020 school year, I began to see the classroom differently. I began to see each of my students differently.

I started to research the Enneagram and the classroom and the Enneagram and parenting. To be honest, there wasn't much content available at the time. There was an insane amount of information on the Enneagram and the different types, but nothing specifically related to the classroom or teaching. There weren't any educational books that I could find and the information available online was helpful, but it didn't quite check all of the boxes for me. Something was still missing.

So, I started to research and develop the very thing I was after.

In my opinion, every teacher should study the Enneagram and supplement their knowledge with this book. I wish I had a guide like this available to me throughout my time in the classroom. Classroom management and parent interactions are the hardest parts of the job, am I right?

If we had classrooms full of students prepared and eager to learn, teaching would be easy. Parents would be happy. Test scores would be off the charts, year after year.

But that isn't how it works. We don't live in a perfect world.

We get challenging students, tired students, hungry students, abused students, homeless students, orphaned students; we also get happy students, well-adjusted students, eager students. We get quiet students and loud students. Students who try and students who don't. All A students and barely passing students. Students who listen and students who do everything but. And they all fit together to create the large puzzle called school.

In addition to differentiating lesson plans for various levels of learning and implementing accommodations for 504 plans and IEPs, we have to balance personalities, learning styles, and communication styles.

Having a guide on the latter sounded like it could greatly benefit the classroom. So that's what this is. A guide for educators, administrators, and parents to be able to gain a little bit of insight from the behaviors, patterns, and tendencies that students are demonstrating.

We will discuss this in more detail later, but I want to make sure you understand that you cannot, and should not, type a child. We can only understand what drives the different types and recognize different tendencies in children. We can observe and respond to the patterns being displayed. The only person we can truly type is ourselves.

I'm going to warn you, once you learn this you can't unlearn it. Once you know, you know. Don't 'wish you had known this sooner' because truthfully, you don't know what you don't know, and that's okay. But at the same time, once you learn it, you have the responsibility to apply it. Like Ben Parker from Spider-Man says, "with great power comes great responsibility." You'll have the power of knowledge of the Enneagram. You'll also have the responsibility to do something with it; the responsibility to change.

Self-awareness is so important. In order to know and understand others, we must first know and understand ourselves. I encourage you to learn about and discover who you are first. Once you truly understand yourself, you'll be able to see others so much more clearly. It sounds wild, but it's true. However, until you personally become self-aware and understand who you are, you won't have the emotional capacity to truly understand others.

This book dives into each of the Enneagram types from a student perspective. The qualities and characteristics of each type haven't changed. So if you are unsure of your type, you should feel connected to one or more of these chapters. I encourage you to learn more about the types that you feel connected to and focus on the core motivations to discover your true type.

The Enneagram alone is just information. When you dive deep into the discovery of yourself and your type, and you pair that with the knowledge of the complete Enneagram, something magical happens.

You will become a better parent, a better teacher, a better administrator if you take the time to discover who you are. A better you is a better them.

I'm excited to share this information with you and I hope that it improves your home life and/or classroom dynamics. If you're ready to gain a deeper understanding of why your kids and students think, feel, and do the things they do, then keep on reading.

XOXO,

Sarah

The Student Enneagram

Ennea is the Greek number prefix 9. The suffix -gram also comes from the Greek language and means what is written, referring to something written or drawn by a human or a machine.

The Enneagram (pronounced any-a-gram) is a nine-pointed geometric drawing that represents the nine different personality types.

Look at the girls below. They are all wearing sunglasses, but each pair has a different colored lens. These girls can look at the exact same object and see three different variations of that object. What we see or experience is dependent upon our lens or filter.

This analogy perfectly represents the nine different personality types. We can look at the exact same picture or experience the exact same situation and have completely different views or perspectives. Again, our perspective is dependent upon our lens. Our perspective is dependent upon our Enneagram type.

Have you ever made an incorrect assumption about why someone did something? We all have. Being able to understand that we all have different filters or lenses helps us to take a step back and try to see the world from someone else's view.

STUDENT ENNEATYPES (pronounced any-a-type)

1. The Serious and Hard-Working Student
2. The Helping and People-Pleasing Student
3. The Popular and Engaging Student
4. The Unique and Creative Student
5. The Observant and Intelligent Student
6. The Questioning and Loyal Student
7. The High-Energy and Adventurous Student
8. The Opinionated and Confident Student
9. The Calm and Peaceful Student

WHAT IS THE ENNEAGRAM?

The Enneagram is a roadmap to transformation. It reveals the reasons a person thinks, feels, and behaves in a certain way. It provides insight for when we are on the right path or when we are heading in the wrong direction and need to turn around.

The individual growth experienced from this journey will not only transform our lives, but our relationships with others as well.

The purpose of the Enneagram is to wake us up to our true selves. Everyone has two selves: the true self and the false self. The false self is the protective layer; the self that has formed defensive and protective mechanisms. The false self is limiting and blocks the way from reaching our true potential. The false self is what the world has molded and formed us into. The true self is the person we were born and created to be. The true self is who we are under all of the false self-layers; the self that existed before the world got ahold of us.

The Enneagram can help with growth by showing us our current location and giving us directions to find our true self. The Enneagram shows whether or not we are aligned, misaligned, or completely out of alignment. Each type has different levels of health or development. If we are out of alignment, then we are at our worst.

If we are in alignment, then we are at our best. Most people are driving around and going about their day misaligned.

- It's possible to continue driving a car with misaligned tires, but this can cause uneven wear and tear on the tires.
- It's also possible to continue living in a misaligned state, but this can cause wear and tear on personal relationships, dreams, and other areas of life. This can cause unnecessary conflicts, miscommunication, and problems in our lives.

The Enneagram shows what growth looks like for each type and exactly how to achieve it. This tool not only shows us our starting point, but it shows us our destination. Meaning, it doesn't just show us who we are, but it shows us who we can become.

QUALITIES OF EACH ENNEATYPE

Qualities of a 1:
self-disciplined, hard-working, polite, responsible, judgmental, critical

Qualities of a 2:
friendly, complimentary, supportive, nurturing, possessive, needy

Qualities of a 3:
energetic, popular, motivating, positive, ambitious, competitive, superficial

Qualities of a 4:
daydreamer, dramatic, authentic, creative, temperamental, possessive

Qualities of a 5:
observant, wise, investigative, innovative, emotionally detached, stubborn

Qualities of a 6:
compassionate, likable, loyal, trustworthy, anxious, rebellious, cautious

Qualities of a 7:
optimistic, adventurer, joker, entertainer, talkative, avoidant, superficial

Qualities of an 8:
compassionate, confrontational, loyal, protective, blunt, resilient, resourceful

Qualities of a 9:
easy-going, pleasant, cooperative, accommodating, indecisive, passive-aggressive

WHO AM I? WHO ARE YOU?

The Enneagram works. Simply put.

It is the most accurate personality typing system available for understanding who you are and who others are. It helps you understand why you don't get along with some, and why you instantly connect with others. After learning and applying the Enneagram you may find yourself wondering how you ever got along without it. You will be forever changed, in the best way.

The Enneagram can make you feel exposed. It's as though someone is taking a look into the depths of your soul and calling you out on everything. It's thrilling and terrifying at the same time. Thrilling because you can't believe that someone finally understands you. Terrifying because how does a system describe you so well?

Understanding who you are creates the emotional capacity for you to bring more acceptance and compassion into your relationships with others, which is a huge positive both in the classroom and with your children at home. Incorporating the Enneagram in the classroom can increase student productivity when it is used as a communication tool. When you are able to communicate in ways your students hear and understand, then you become a more effective teacher, administrator, and parent.

And isn't that the goal?

You see, you can say something to your kids, but just because the words leave your mouth, doesn't mean they are being received or understood. Each Enneagram type has preferred communication methods, strengths, and weaknesses. You've done the work to learn whether your students learn visually, auditorily, or kinesthetically, now it's time to take that ten steps further.

According to Enneagram Scholar Rob Fitzel, "When we study nine personality types of the Enneagram, we can better understand how and why others see the world differently from us. This awareness leads to greater compassion and acceptance of others. We can apply this knowledge to adapt our teaching style (sometimes in very small ways) to make a big difference in how well our students learn. In the classroom, the Enneagram can help teachers and students connect to be effective partners in education."

The Enneagram will be your secret weapon. Once you recognize patterns and behaviors in your children and your students, you will be able to understand how to connect with them and engage with them in ways that will make them feel seen, heard, and valued.

THE ENNEAGRAM + CHILDREN

I mentioned this in the introduction and now I want to dive a little bit deeper: we cannot and should not type a child. I need to make it very clear that typing children is not a good idea. And when I say "not a good idea," I mean it could be detrimental to their development. So please don't type them.

Children aren't mature enough to truly understand their core motivations. Some young adults may be able to identify their type in their late teenage years, for others it may take until their twenties.

High school teachers may be able to give their students Enneagram assessments as long as they let their students know that the assessment is a starting point for a journey of self-discovery. Teachers and students in these cases should not lean on the online assessment results solely. (I have classroom specific assessments available on my website – www.sarahwaxman.coach)

I recommend really digging in and learning about all of the types, that way you can recognize behaviors and tendencies children display. You can then navigate your interactions with different children based on the tendencies they present in their day to day, but as far as labeling them or telling them that they are a certain type, don't do it.

Our personalities are typically set by the age of 5 or 6. Many Enneagram teachers believe that we are born with our dominant type and that it influences how nature, nurture, and early childhood are experienced. Each Enneagram type reacts to and perceives situations differently. If a child is a One, nothing from childhood made that child a One. They were born a One. Just like they were born with a certain color eye or character trait. Also, our core motivations don't change throughout our lives, so we aren't one type as a child and then another as an adult. We have one dominant type and that's our type for life.

Because children don't always have the capacity to completely understand what drives them, they aren't able to determine their type yet. In addition, each type has a stress path and a growth path. A child can easily be in an unhealthy level of development and lean heavily into their stress path, which would cause them to show tendencies of that type instead of their true dominant type.

As of the publish date, my oldest is 8. I know what tendencies he is displaying, but he doesn't, and I am not going to tell him. I am, however, going to parent him based on the information I know about that Enneagram type. If I told him, not only would that take away his opportunity to discover himself when he is older, but I could put him into a box and provide him with an excuse for some of the behaviors he displays. And worse, I could be wrong.

We all have each type within us. We have strong connections with some types, and hardly any connection at all with others. But there is one single dominant type, and that is our main Enneagram type. Just because a child demonstrates Type Six behaviors, doesn't mean they will grow up to be a Type Six adult. On the other hand, they very well may grow up to be a Type Six adult. The point is, we don't know because kids aren't adults yet. We don't know what their core motivations are, and chances are, they don't either.

Many believe that kids are the ones who need to change, when really, it's us - the adults. As I said, I know what type my oldest is currently displaying. If it changes as he moves in and out of times of stress and growth and he begins to demonstrate other type tendencies, then my techniques and communication patterns will change with him. That's our job as parents and teachers, adjust and meet our kids where they are.

THE STRUCTURE + WINGS

The Enneagram is a nine-pointed geometric figure. Each Enneatype is shown at the circle where two lines meet. These meeting points are represented by the different colored circles. This diagram specifically represents Type One. In this diagram, and the others that follow in each section, you'll see two arrows pointing in different directions from the colored circle, or the Enneatype. These arrows represent the paths and directions that each type leans in to when they are in stress and when they are demonstrating growth. I will discuss these arrows and paths in each type specific section. In addition, each Enneatype is connected to a total of four types and can tap into the characteristics and qualities of those types. In this example, Type One is connected to Types Two, Four, Seven and Nine, and has the ability to draw from the positive and negative characteristics and qualities of each of these types. Each Enneagram type has access to two paths and two wings. The curved arrows represent the wings, and the straight arrows represent the paths.

The wings for Type One are Types Two and Nine. The wings are like the cream and sugar in a cup of coffee.

Some people prefer more cream. Some people prefer more sugar. Some people prefer just one or the other. Most of us use both cream and sugar to some degree, just as we are able to access both of our wings. Depending on the situation or environment we are in, we are more likely to pull from one wing over the other. We have access to both, and at our healthiest, we are pulling from the positive characteristics of each wing.

LEVELS OF DEVELOPMENT

Just as we are able to access four other types on the Enneagram, our dominant type has various levels of development or health. I typically refer to these levels as being aligned, misaligned, or out of alignment in my coaching sessions and workshops. But to keep it simple, I'll use the words healthy, average, and unhealthy throughout this book.

When we are healthy, we are tapping into the best and most positive traits that our type has to offer. To be the healthiest version of ourselves, we are also accessing the healthiest traits of both of our wings and both of our arrows. It's quite a mountain to climb to get to that level of health, but it is possible.

Most kids and adults are going to be in the average range of health. They aren't going to be their best all the time, but they aren't going to be their worst either.I would like to note that I am not a licensed medical or mental health professional. I am not a counselor, therapist, psychologist, psychiatrist, etc. I am a certified Enneagram coach. When discussing the levels of development or health throughout this book, my intent is to provide information, so parents, teachers, and administrators are aware of the negative behaviors and tendencies of each type. In unhealth, kids and adults alike can suffer from a variety of disorders, drug, and alcohol abuse, suicidal thoughts, etc. I can't emphasize enough that this book is not to diagnose or treat these unhealthy behaviors, but to open your eyes to the patterns so the adults in a child's life can seek out professional help.

If you feel that your child or student is in an unhealthy area and demonstrating troubling behaviors, don't go into panic mode. Take a deep and relaxing breath, figure out what may be triggering them, and seek professional help.

Now, let's take a closer look at what the levels of development actually mean.

While there are only nine personality types on the Enneagram, each type can look very different. The levels of development are the reason behind these differences, and they show us how people change during different seasons or stages of life. Below is the scale created by Enneagram teachers Don Riso and Russ Hudson in the 1990s.

THE LEVELS OF DEVELOPMENT SCALE

Healthy
- Level 1 - The Level of Liberation
- Level 2 - The Level of Psychological Capacity
- Level 3 - The Level of Social Value

Average
- Level 4 - The Level of Imbalance or Social Role
- Level 5 - The Level of Interpersonal Control
- Level 6 - The Level of Overcompensation

Unhealthy
- Level 7 - The Level of Violation
- Level 8 - The Level of Obsession and Compulsion
- Level 9 - The Level of Pathological Destructiveness

Psychological shifts occur at each level on this scale. For example, at level 5, the Level of Interpersonal Control, in order to get psychological needs met, a person may manipulate themselves and others. This would naturally cause interpersonal conflicts.

If the manipulation tactics at level 5 do not work, the anxiety may increase causing them to fall to level 6, the Level of Overcompensation. At this level, the behavior may become more intrusive and aggressive. This person is still trying to get their needs met, regardless of how their behavior and attitude impacts others around them.

Attempting to understand the level of development can provide mental health professionals with a baseline so they can help and support their clients. This provides them with a better opportunity to offer solutions.

THE CENTERS OF INTELLIGENCE

Heart Center

Types Two, Three, and Four belong to the Heart Center or Feeling Triad. These types heavily rely on their emotions and want to be valuable and significant. They share a common emotional struggle: shame.

Twos try to compensate for their shame by getting others to like them. Twos desire to feel wanted, needed, loved, and appreciated. They do this by convincing themselves that they are good and loving because of all of the help and support they give to others. They focus on their positive feelings and repress their negative feelings. If Twos get the positive responses from others that they seek, then they have achieved their goal; they feel wanted, needed, loved, and appreciated.

Threes try to deny their shame. They develop a coping strategy to deal with their shame by turning themselves into what they believe someone who is valued and successful is like. Because of this, Threes learn to perform and deliver. They want to be, or appear to be, the best. They are internally driven and motivated to achieve and find success in hopes that they don't come face to face with humiliation, failure, or shame.

Fours try to avoid their shame by shifting focus to their character traits and to how special and unique they are. Fours are the most likely type to give in to mediocrity and feelings of inadequacy. Fours want to be authentic and real, and they focus on their creativity and individuality instead of dealing with any shameful feelings that may arise. Fours also have wonderful imaginations. Another way they avoid shame is to imagine a fantasy life that eliminates the parts of their lives that are boring or mundane.

These three types are driven by their emotions, and they typically rely on their feelings to help guide them when they make decisions.

These types are known for wearing their hearts on their sleeves.

THE CENTERS OF INTELLIGENCE
Head Center

Types Five, Six, and Seven belong to the Head Center or Thinking Triad. These types share characteristics such as analytical thinking and anxiety in social situations. They focus on remaining in their comfort zone. They share a common emotional struggle: anxiety.

Fives struggle with anxiety about how much time and energy they have to devote to the outer world and social situations. In response to this, they withdraw and isolate themselves from the world. They can become secretive and keep their personal lives private. Fives want to be competent and capable. They hope to eventually join in and participate with others, but they never feel like they have enough information to confidently move from spectator to participant.

Sixes struggle with anxiety in general. Sixes are out of touch with their confidence and intellect. They don't trust themselves and they constantly seek validation and answers from those they look up to. They desire certainty, security, and guidance. They need reassurance from others to be sure of themselves and their decisions. It doesn't matter how many people they have in their inner circle to guide them; they still feel anxious and doubtful of their abilities. They aren't sure of anything. They constantly question themselves.

Sevens struggle with anxiety about themselves. Sevens want to avoid serious and painful emotions and situations. The coping strategy they developed to deal with this is to keep themselves occupied with the next exciting thing. As long as they have something exciting to look forward to, they can escape the painful feelings and distract themselves from their fears. Oftentimes Sevens find that they miss out on the present because they are always thinking about the next adventure. They keep themselves entertained with a long list of experiences and activities to do.

THE CENTERS OF INTELLIGENCE
Body Center

Types Eight, Nine, and One belong to the Body Center or the Instinctive Triad. These types heavily rely on their instincts or gut feelings. They want everything to be just and fair. They share a common emotional struggle: anger.

When Eights get angry, they are not afraid to show it. They easily and readily let their anger out. When Eights feel themselves getting angry, or they feel anger building up within them, they immediately respond to it. They aren't the type to mess around. They will act in some sort of physical way: a raised voice, forceful movement, changed body language and facial expressions, and so on. They give themselves permission to express their anger, and others clearly notice when Eights are upset. They don't keep it inside.

Nines are quite the opposite. They deny their anger. They like to believe that they aren't able to be angered. Of all of the Enneagram types, Nines are the ones who are not in touch with their anger. Nines choose peace and harmony over conflict and tension. They would rather stay out of a situation and enjoy a seemingly unrealistic and peaceful world than be angry or find themselves in conflict. But don't let them fool you, they can and will get angry if they've reached their limit.

Ones get angry, but they try to repress it because they are focused on being good, balanced, and right. Anger destroys that balance. Ones feel that they need to be in control of their emotions and impulses. If they aren't in control, then they aren't being good. Their 'inner critic' keeps them in check. They would prefer to hide and bury their anger as opposed to getting angry and then, consequently, getting berated by their 'inner critic.'

These three types struggle with anger and they struggle differently. They typically rely on their instincts and their gut to make decisions.

ENNEAGRAM TYPE ONE
The Serious & Hard-Working Student

*"Stand up and face the future, stand up and be the change.
You don't have to fear forever, don't have to be afraid.
If we can stand together, then we can make it right.
If we can fight the battle, love will win it every time."*

- Be The Change, Lily-Jo

reliable
productive
fair
judgmental
inflexible
responsible
honest
ethical

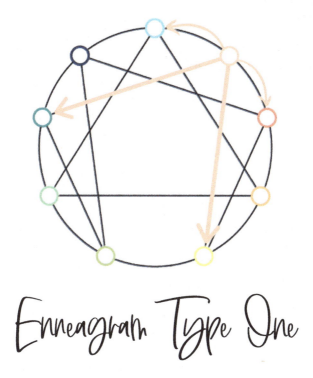

Enneagram Type One

Ones always want to do what is right and fair. They pride themselves on being reliable, hard-working, and someone who is an excellent example for others. Ones find comfort in structure and following guidelines. Because of this, they are honest, dependable, and are constantly striving to be the best version of themselves. Ones are severely critical of themselves and are heavily burdened by the voice of their 'inner critic,' which criticizes them constantly.

Ones want things to be correct in all situations, so they are often giving advice on how to improve, which can be interpreted by others as judgmental and hurtful. A One's commitment to the 'right way' of doing things guides their thoughts and behavior.

Ones feel that they are on a mission, and they must be serious, determined, and committed so they don't waste time. This can cause them to be very strict and rigid with themselves and others.

Ones would love to be more adventurous and relaxed, but the voice of their 'inner critic' often prohibits them from being able to enjoy life. Oftentimes, they only time a One is able to relax and let loose is when they are on vacation, or for students specifically, during any sort of break from school when the pressure is off.

Many types desire to achieve, but Ones are aware of how they achieve. Did they achieve their goal honorably? Were they wise with their choices and resources? Were they fair? Were they honest and truthful? Did they play by the rules?

Ones have high standards, and they expect the best from themselves and from others.

IN A NUTSHELL...

The Type One student is a perfectionist. In fact, they may want to avoid failure. So much so, that they won't even attempt something new. If they believe they won't be successful, they will shy away to avoid negative feedback from their 'inner critic.'

Core Fear - Being bad, wrong, or defective; making mistakes
Core Desire - To always be good and correct
Focus - This is wrong. This isn't right. This needs to be perfected.
Goal - To follow rules and guidelines so that they always meet (or exceed) expectations.

Biggest Struggle - Resentment

Ones typically repress their anger which leads to frustration, irritation, and not being satisfied with themselves and others.

CHARACTERISTICS

Ones are self-disciplined and they are mature and polite for their age. They are natural teachers, and they have a very strong sense of right and wrong. They are responsible and ethical, and they want to be perceived as hard-working students who always do the right thing.

Ones believe that there is only one right way to do things, and if something is worth doing, it needs to be done well. Ones won't do something halfway. Ones are very observant and may look for opportunities to point out and correct others' mistakes. They notice things that are incorrect or out of place.

While Ones may appear to be sure of themselves, deep down they may lack confidence. They sometimes struggle to believe that they can live up to their incredibly high standards. Because of this, they can isolate themselves. They sometimes feel burdened by the thought that others won't perform as well or put forth as much effort as they do. If this thought process continues, they can become extremely harsh and critical of themselves and others.

COMMUNICATION STYLE

Ones are direct and to the point. They are very detail-oriented. They are focused on the topic at hand and do not like when others interrupt or change the subject if they are discussing something important. They have strong morals and values, and they believe that honesty, objectivity, and integrity are what matter most. Ones are very serious and hard-working. Their tone may sound judgy or overly critical at times.

Below are a few suggestions on how to effectively communicate with a Serious and Hard-Working Student:

- Praise them. If they did something correctly, let them know. They talk down to themselves on a regular basis, a little outside praise goes a long way in boosting their confidence.
- Ones like clear and direct communication, but they don't like conflict. They will initiate hard conversations (if they need to), but it's only so that things are sorted out and understood.
- Keep in mind, they aren't trying to be judgmental and critical. They need things to be perfect and they are quick to notice imperfections and mistakes.
- Take them seriously.
- Apologize when you make a mistake. This shows the One that everyone makes mistakes and teaches them that it's okay to make mistakes. Ones are human, too.
- Encourage and support Ones by showing them multiple ways to get things done or solve a problem.

LEARNING STYLE

Ones are excellent listeners and very detail-oriented. They like clear and concise directions, and they want to make sure they know and understand every rule and procedure. They take their learning extremely seriously and will oftentimes double or triple-check their work to make sure they haven't made any mistakes or skipped over something accidentally.

Ones are going to be motivated by getting good grades. An A+ quiets their 'inner critic.' As long as the directions are clear, they know exactly what they need to do to achieve good grades or turn in high-quality work. Nothing less than perfect will suffice.

WORK ETHIC

As mentioned previously, Ones pay serious attention to detail. They are the planners and list makers. They are dedicated to the task and complete tasks accurately and perfectly. They work until the project is finished. Ones can sometimes have a difficult time stopping a project and coming back to it later. If they sit down to do something, they are going to do it and do it well. They are their own worst critic, so not doing something well, or making a mistake, is devastating.

Ones actually love group work, if everyone in the group puts in the same amount of effort. Ones do not like when others cut corners or don't take the project as seriously as they do.

Report card feedback may say: Student is very conscientious, student struggles with feedback, or student is a real asset to the classroom.

PREFERRED CLASSROOM ENVIRONMENT

Ones prefer to be around people who are like them: responsible, self-disciplined, and conscientious. They need an organized environment and a classroom setting where not only their teacher is prepared for the day, but the students are also prepared mentally and physically. They don't understand why someone would come to class unprepared or why a teacher would not have a well-planned lesson.

They need the classroom rules and procedures to be fair and appropriate, but more importantly, the teacher needs to be consistent in enforcing the rules. The same rule needs to apply to each student, regardless of the situation or circumstance.

Remind Ones that perfection cannot be reached. Reassure them that perfection does not exist. They are hypercritical of themselves and their work. If they make a mistake, they could shut down which could hinder their learning.

While their grades may not reflect it, some One students find school difficult and tiring because they have to work so hard.

WINGS

The wings attached to Type One are The Helping and People-Pleasing Student (Type Two) and The Calm and Peaceful Student (Type Nine). These wings can be abbreviated as 1W9 and 1W2.

THE 1W9

The Type One with the Nine wing tends to be cooler, more relaxed, cerebral, introverted, gentle, impersonal, objective, and detached from their emotions. When they are struggling, they are more subdued and impatient. They may speak with a more judgmental tone. This wing is inspiring because they are able to make others aware of what's wrong by expressing the problem or issue in ways that are easy to understand.

THE 1W2

The Type One with the Two wing tends to be warmer, more vocal, social, helpful, sensitive, controlling, and action-oriented. When they are struggling, they are more vocal with their advice and insist that others follow it. They can overstep their boundaries. This wing is inspiring because they are able to see what's wrong, but instead of criticizing, they jump right in and help to solve the problem.

THINGS TO LEARN

Ones would benefit from learning how to pace themselves and understanding that it is okay to complete work in chunks. They do not have to sit down to a project and complete it in its entirety in a single session. They can learn that it's okay to: be angry, open, and honest, have fun and relax, make mistakes, and be spontaneous.

IN STRESS

In stress, a One moves towards an average to an unhealthy Type Four. They will become resentful and angry when things aren't going as planned or when people aren't meeting their expectations. They can withdraw or isolate when they are feeling misunderstood so they can work through and process their emotions alone. They may begin to daydream about being a different person or having a different life, one in which they are able to just be themselves. When Ones are struggling, they are more likely to believe that others don't understand them and may spend a lot of time explaining themselves.

IN GROWTH

In growth, a One moves towards a healthy Type Seven. They will begin to experience more joy, peace, and compassion which will turn them away from their natural judgmental state. They will become more optimistic, spontaneous, and fun. Ones in growth will be able to take a step back and recognize that others are most likely giving and trying their best. This will help them to become less rigid. They will be able to feel more relaxed and realize that life doesn't have to be so serious, all the time.

LEVELS OF DEVELOPMENT

Healthy levels:

Level 1 - (at their best) They are extremely wise. They become completely realistic when they are able to accept 'what is,' which allows them to recognize the best action to take in each situation. They are motivating and hopeful.

Level 2 - They have strong personal convictions and are extremely grounded in their belief of what's right and wrong. They have strong values and morals. They desire to be rational, reasonable, self-disciplined, and mature.

Level 3 - They always want to be fair and objective. Ethics, justice, and truth are at the top of their list of values. They strive to demonstrate responsibility and integrity, which often makes them the go-to person for the truth.

Average levels:

Level 4 - They aren't content with their current reality. They feel that it is their job to make everything perfect. They feel like they need to explain to others how things 'should be' and make sure that others follow through on all of the improvments and suggestions.

Level 5 - They are workaholics and are afraid to make mistakes. Everything must be perfect, in order, and consistent with their beliefs. They are organized but are also restricted emotionally.

Level 6 - They are perfectionists and extremely critical of themselves and others. They are judgmental and opinionated about everything. They constantly correct others and nag them if things aren't done 'the right way.' They are seriously impatient, abrasive, and angry when life doesn't match their ideals.

Unhealthy levels:

Level 7 - They are highly self-righteous, intolerant of others, and unaccommodating. They are 'right' about everything and everyone else is wrong. They are extremely judgmental and find ways to justify their actions.

Level 8 - They obsess over imperfections of themselves and others and mistakes others make. They can become hypocritical and do things opposite of what they tell others to do.

Level 9 - Depression, nervous breakdowns, anxiety, and self-harming behaviors are possible. They condemn and are cruel towards others. They eliminate anyone who doesn't fit their perfect mold. They can suffer from OCD and other depressive personality disorders.

DEFENSE MECHANISM

The defense mechanism for the One is reaction formation. Ones have high standards for themselves and for others. They believe that they must remain in control of their emotions, otherwise they will not display an image of being good. Keeping their emotions and behaviors in check is a top priority. In order to do this, Ones will oftentimes hide or conceal what they are truly feeling anddemonstrate the opposite. They may feel angry about something, but they will remain unaffected. They may feel overworked, but will continue pushing forward to get whatever task finished. They may feel jealous of someone else's achievement, but will praise and congratulate them. Their 'inner critic' demands them to always be good and do good. This can cause them to neglect their true thoughts, feelings, and emotions, and deny their own personal needs.

CHILDHOOD PATTERNS

One children are focused on obeying the rules and mostly keep to themselves. Their 'inner critic' shows up early in childhood and is just as much of a burden to the One as a child as it is for an adult. A One child does not need much direction or correction from authority figures. However, when the One child is disciplined, they heavily internalize it along with the criticism they are already carrying. The One child does not take risks or seek activities that they are unfamiliar with. They do not multitask well since every task in their mind has to be done perfectly. The One child is more comfortable in spaces that are organized and free of chaos. As a result, the One child (typically) prefers to keep their room clean and does not have to be reminded to do so by a parent or guardian.

TRIGGERS FOR CONFLICT

When Ones are triggered, they may start to speak with a sharp tone of voice and become critical. They may bring up unrelated problems and issues and become rigid and adamant that their expectations and standards are met. Pay attention to their nonverbal cues: a tight jaw, pursed lips, and a tense upper body.

Conflict in Ones may be triggered by someone criticizing them. If a One sees someone else being lazy or irresponsible, they may feel triggered because they personally aren't lazy or irresponsible and they don't understand how other people can be. Those things aren't 'good' or 'right.' Ones don't like when other people are deceptive or misleading. A big trigger for a One is when they feel that other people are not taking responsibility or doing their fair share of the work.

A HOW-TO GUIDE FOR THE SERIOUS AND HARD-WORKING STUDENT

- Don't be too hard on your One student. They are already hyper-aware of their mistakes and the last thing they need is to be told that they made a mistake. Keep in mind that they are already harder on themselves than you will be on them.
- Focus and praise the positive qualities in your student.
- One children really try their best to do the right thing all of the time. Let them know that they are doing a great job and are good students and role models.
- It's important to pay attention to their level of development:
    - A healthy Type One is extremely grounded, reasonable, mature, and responsible. They are able to accept situations for what they are.
    - An average Type One tries to make everything perfect. They feel like they always need to explain how things should be done. They work really hard and are terrified to make a mistake. They are very critical of themselves and others.
    - An unhealthy Type One is intolerable of others. They believe that they are always right and obsess over the mistakes that others make. They do this to take the pressure off of themselves. If a student is at a healthy level, encourage and reassure them that they are on the right path.
- If a student is at an unhealthy level, pay attention to their environment. What may be triggering their negative behaviors and attitudes? Find ways to work with their strengths and make them more confident.
- Pushing, nagging, or focusing on their mistakes and flaws will more than likely only make matters worse. If needed, seek professional help and guidance.

FAMOUS ENNEAGRAM ONES

- Nelson Mandela
- Tina Fey
- Eleanor Roosevelt
- Brene Brown
- Steve Jobs
- Captain "Sully" Sullenberger
- Mahatma Gandhi
- Hermione Granger (*Harry Potter*)

TYPE ONE QUESTIONNAIRE

Does the student:

- seem to have a loud voice in their head that constantly tells them what they need to do or how they can improve without you needing to tell them?

- help with classroom chores or jobs without being asked?

- think they know everything and correct others without hesitation?

- give advice on how to be more organized and/or clean?

- frequently ask you if they are a good boy/girl?

- take school seriously and struggle to understand those who don't?

- feel like everything needs to be perfect before it is finished?

- correct mistakes made by teachers and peers?

- try to control their peers, but not in a negative or bullying type of way?

- engage in adult conversation easily, but struggle to play with other kids?

ADULT REFLECTIONS ON BEING A SERIOUS AND HARD-WORKING STUDENT

1. I was very studious. I sat upright and always tucked in my chair. I sat quietly in my seat, and I did not misbehave in class. I aced my tests and loved to get called on because I answered the questions correctly.
2. I couldn't stand the kids in my classes who misbehaved. It made it hard for the teacher to teach.
3. I was a top student and some people called me a teacher's pet. I was okay with that.
4. I always followed the rules. I took honors and AP level classes. I was an excellent student.
5. I made straight As, but I was also up all hours of the night studying. Any grade below an A was not good enough.
6. Sometimes I didn't do projects because I knew I wouldn't be able to do them perfectly. My test grades made up for those zeros, though. My grades were decent.
7. I was a talker, but my teachers still loved me. I always raised my hand to answer questions and I worked hard to get good grades.
8. My parents didn't have to worry about me getting into trouble. I was a straight-A student and a complete goody-two-shoes.
9. I was so focused on grades and homework that I didn't really have much of a social life. I was friendly and I had a lot of friends at school, but we never really got together outside of school or sports.
10. I loved sports, but I wasn't a super competitive athlete. I made sure I did my best, and if I messed up, I would beat myself up over it for a while, but I didn't really get upset if my team lost.

WHAT BEING A SERIOUS AND HARD-WORKING STUDENT WAS LIKE:

As a student, I never struggled in the traditional sense. My parents never had to ask me if I'd completed my homework, nor did they have to push me to achieve. I chose to only take upper-level courses - AP, if offered, and I made straight As.

By the end of the 9th grade, I'd completed all college math. My teachers loved me and would often ask to keep my projects and papers as an example for future classes. Praise from my teachers motivated me. I enjoyed all subjects but would become easily frustrated by students who disrupted class. Teachers who were more laid-back and lacked structure frustrated me. I would often ask for clarification on expectations, and after work was graded, I was disappointed when feedback wasn't provided.

I spent several hours studying every night, but not because I was struggling to learn the material. I didn't just want an A average, I wanted every test, every assignment, and every class average to be an A+. Because of this drive for perfection, I struggled with crippling test anxiety. While I knew the material, I would question myself and whether or not I'd worked hard enough to truly know the right answer. To try to compensate, I would spend hours quizzing myself on material in an attempt to prepare.

Outside of the classroom, I was actively involved in many clubs and was a member of multiple honor societies including: National Honor Society, French National Honor Society, Mu Alpha Theta, and the international Thespian Society. Additionally, I was a principal actor for our school's theatre program. When I wasn't studying for my classes, I was rehearsing for theatre. I loved school, but my drive for perfection exhausted me.

- **Sara Burns, 1W9**

As a student, grades were incredibly important to me except for when they weren't. If a subject or position was something I was passionate about, I worked to be the very best. If it wasn't - or more importantly if I didn't think it was RIGHT - then I would not.

My sense of justice and right and wrong was always more pronounced than those around me. If I felt like a teacher was not good, or treated some students unfairly, I would not do my best in class - even though I was an honors student.

While my grades in all subjects, except math, were very high, my work in high school with the school newspaper was my proudest accomplishment. I was known for scathing editorials about anything that seemed wrong to me.

I recall one specific series I completed about our guidance department. The students complained that if they did not get good grades and seem like 'college material,' our guidance department did not give them as much attention and support. Even though I was a student who did receive support from the guidance department, it was wrong that not everyone received the attention they needed. I wrote a lengthy editorial for our paper, which caused a lot of stirs. While this was the biggest moment, my whole educational career was spent in smaller battles for justice. Making things right was always my biggest driving force.

- **Kelley S., 1W2**

I wanted to do well in school. What's the point of doing something if you aren't going to give it your best shot? I wasn't the smartest kid in my class, but I always made decent grades, even in the classes I didn't like. I always gave my best effort.

I was a well-behaved kid - at school and at home, but especially at home. I did not want to get in trouble. I got in trouble a few times that I can remember, once in 4th grade and once in 9th grade. It didn't happen frequently because I knew better. Again, what's the point of doing something if you aren't going to give it your best shot? It just never occurred to me that I didn't have to try or listen. I had to give it my best. I had to follow the rules and directions I was given.

I dressed well for school. My shirt was always tucked in because that's what you were supposed to do. That's how you were supposed to dress (I graduated high school in 1972). I didn't want to go to school, or anywhere really, if I wasn't put together. Each night before school I would lay my clothes and school materials out so I knew that I had everything I needed for the next day. My bedroom was probably the cleanest room in the house.

I was well liked and had a lot of friends, except for when I made the *varsity basketball team as a freshman and started over the senior boys, they didn't care for me. I lived for basketball. I was always practicing, and I didn't go anywhere without a ball in my hand.*

- **male, 1W2**

ENNEAGRAM TYPE TWO
The Helping & People-Pleasing Student

"I'll be your eyes 'til yours can shine.
And I'll be your arms, I'll be your steady satellite.
And when you can't rise, well
I'll crawl with you on hands and knees
'cause I'm gonna stand by you."

- Stand By You, Rachel Platten

nurturing

supportive

friendly

needy

manipulative

compassionate

generous

warm

Enneagram Type Two

When a Two is at their best, they are encouraging, loving, full of joy, humble, forgiving, incorporate self-care into their day, and show grace to themselves and others.

At their worst, they flatter others to get their way. They can be manipulative and possessive. They are clingy, needy, and do what they need to do in order to please others.

When Twos don't have clear boundaries, they can have a hard time saying "no," and they find it difficult to draw a line when it comes to taking care of others. When a Two is at their best, they have clear boundaries and recognize when to say "no" without feeling guilty.

A struggling Two will insert themselves into the lives of others, with or without permission. They believe that if they offer help, support, or guidance, then others will appreciate and need them. They will be wanted. They won't be rejected. When the Two gives unsolicited help or advice, others will attempt to create boundaries for them. This leaves the Two feeling hurt and insecure about the relationship which could lead to feeling rejected.

Twos believe that they have to be needed before they can be loved and they have to give before they can get. When they doubt that others love or want them, they will double the effort to win people over. They get caught in a cycle of people-pleasing and constantly look for things to do or say that will get others to like them.

Twos like to talk about their relationships with people. This is a regular topic of conversation because twos need constant reassurance that their relationships are secure and stable.

Twos are the most people-focused of the Enneagram types.

IN A NUTSHELL...

The Two student is a people-pleaser. They are focused on helping others because they believe that their help and support is the only reason their peers and teachers like them. They will often dismiss their needs and take care of others first.

Core Fear - Inadequacy, not being needed, loved or appreciated
Core Desire - To be loved, appreciated, and wanted
Focus - How can they help? What do others need?
Goal - Be kind and helpful to others in order to feel loved and appreciated.

Biggest Struggle – Pride

Twos typically deny their own needs and emotions and use their intense intuition to understand the emotions and needs of others. Then, they confidently insert themselves to offer help and support in hopes that others will appreciate them and want them around.

CHARACTERISTICS

Twos are extremely empathetic and sincere. They are self-sacrificing and generous with their time, energy, and space. They are the students who will give their lunch to the child who is hungry.

Twos truly want to connect with others in a heartfelt way and they want to be a source of love and kindness for others. They feel best about themselves when they have meaningful relationships. They love sharing the good things about their lives and genuinely want to support others when they are in need.

COMMUNICATION STYLE

Twos are very relationship-focused and live to serve others. They value communication and appreciate eye contact. Positive reinforcement goes a long way because Twos desire to be valued and appreciated. Thanking them or letting them know that they did a great job is a confidence booster and will keep them engaged and motivated. They value relationships with others over anything else. Twos are incredible friends.

Twos may compromise their learning in order to preserve a relationship or their helpful image. You can trust that when a Two offers to help with something it is well-intentioned, because, most of the time, they genuinely want to help. If their eagerness to assist starts to feel overwhelming, thank them for their assistance and the effort they have demonstrated. Acknowledge that they are thoughtful and caring, and ask if they can give you some space and time to work independently.

Below are a few suggestions on how to effectively communicate with a Helping and People-Pleasing Student:

- To really strike up a conversation, ask more than a general "How are you?"
- Reassure Twos that self-care is important and that it's okay to say "no," have boundaries, and take a break for themselves.
- Let them know how much you appreciate the little things they do.
- Twos want deep connections with their peers. They welcome honesty and vulnerability.
- Twos may not openly ask for help, but they appreciate and want people to help them, too.

LEARNING STYLE

Twos enjoy a lesson that taps into their emotions. When they are able to make an emotional connection to the material, they are more interested in learning. They are focused on the needs of their classmates and strive to help both teachers and students when given the opportunity. They find role models and mentors in their school to look up to and learn from.

Twos need clear and specific directions when it comes to an individual assignment versus working with a group. Twos love to mentor and coach others. Oftentimes, they will volunteer to help struggling students, as long as the Two is confident in the material.

Twos desire to be needed and appreciated. Putting them in a position to help will boost their confidence and their learning.

WORK ETHIC

Twos adapt to classroom situations and teachers' differences and preferences easily to gain approval. They desire to earn good grades and make their teacher happy. As mentioned above, Twos love to volunteer to help; whether that is to help tutor other students or help the classroom teacher with day-to-day tasks.

They are sensitive to criticism and take feedback personally. They see a disagreement as disapproval. They always try to give their best effort, so they gain approval from others and are seen as more valuable classroom contributors.

Report card feedback may say: Student is pleasant and friendly towards others, student is too dependent on the teacher, or student always gives their best effort.

PREFERRED CLASSROOM ENVIRONMENT

If you need a classroom helper, ask a Two student. They will feel needed, wanted, and appreciated, which is their ultimate desire. Twos enjoy emotional connections and appreciate thoughtfulness in others. They aren't going to be the first to admit they need help, but they appreciate it when others assist them. Twos struggle when they give, and give, and give, and their efforts aren't recognized or reciprocated.

They need a mutually supportive environment where both students and teachers are actively engaged and help to support each other. These students love group work and whole-group discussion. They are people-people, and they enjoy the company of others and the connection that comes with it.

Remind Twos that they are appreciated, even if they aren't doing something for someone else. Twos believe that in order to be loved and valued, they have to do something to earn it. This is why they constantly offer assistance and support to others. They want to be included and they want to have meaningful relationships.

WINGS

The wings attached to Type Two are The Serious and Hard-Working Student (Type One) and The Popular and Engaging Student (Type Three). These wings can be abbreviated as 2W1 and 2W3.

THE 2W1

The Type Two with the One wing is serious and objective, and they have more control over their emotions. They have a strong sense of responsibility to always do the right thing. They quietly serve behind the scenes and don't necessarily want or need attention or praise. When they are struggling, they can be more insistent, controlling, and demanding that others follow their advice. The 2W1 is an excellent teacher. This wing is inspiring because they focus on truly improving the lives of others through nurturing them and caring for them.

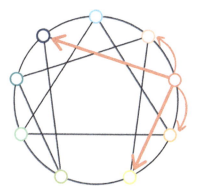

THE 2W3

The Type Two with the Three wing tends to be more outgoing, sociable, affirming, and self-assured. They bless others with their gifts and talents. The Twos biggest gift is their heart. They want to be admired and they focus on being likable and successful. When they are struggling, they can become obsessed with getting approval and receiving affirmation and praise from others. This wing is inspiring because they are very outgoing and charming, and they enjoy living in the spotlight.

THINGS TO LEARN

Twos would benefit from learning that they really are loved for who they are; that they don't need to do anything in order to be loved. They need to learn that they are allowed to say "no," establish boundaries, and that it is important for them to take care of themselves. While it may be tough, Twos need to figure out what they need and learn how to be comfortable sharing and expressing their needs with others.

IN STRESS

In stress, a Two moves towards an average to an unhealthy Type Eight. Unhealthy Twos, or stressed Twos, become needy, irritable, aggressive, blunt, and dominating. They place blame and demands on others, and they try to control others and situations. They can become defensive if they feel that they are being ignored or rejected. Struggling Twos may become confrontational or make threats to take away their support and help from others. They may start to manipulate others into doing the things they want. Twos can avoid taking responsibility for their actions and instead, blame others and give excuses as to why things aren't their fault.

IN GROWTH

In growth, a Two moves towards a healthy Type Four. Type Twos become more nurturing and compassionate towards themselves. They become more emotionally aware and are able to process difficult feelings, as well as accept and admit them. They are aware that they tell themselves that their motives are always pure, because deep down, they realize they are not. They are able to see themselves, the good and the bad, and ask for forgiveness. When Twos are growing, they realize that they are wanted and loved, regardless of what they do for others.

LEVELS OF DEVELOPMENT

Healthy levels:

Level 1 - (at their best) These Twos are the most unselfish and humble people around. They give unconditional love to both themselves and others. They are blessed to be in the lives of others.
Level 2 - They are extremely caring, compassionate, and concerned about others. They are empathetic, thoughtful, sincere, and forgiving.
Level 3 - They see the good in others and give others the benefit of the doubt. They are encouraging and appreciative. They live to serve others but know that they also need to care for themselves. They are generous, giving, and extremely loving.

Average levels:

Level 4 - They want to be loved. They become overly friendly and do what they think someone will like in order to gain their affection and approval. They people-please in an attempt to be closer to others.
Level 5 - They are helicopters. They need to be needed so they hover. They want others to depend on them. They give but expect something in return. They are possessive and can't say no to others. They self-sacrifice to the detriment of their own needs, wants, and even health. They constantly seek to serve others, which in turn wears them out and empties their cup.
Level 6 - They believe they cannot be replaced. They are presumptuous and overbearing. They give themselves too much credit for their efforts.

Unhealthy levels:

Level 7 - They can be self-serving. They make others suffer from feeling guilty. They are manipulative and can undermine others. They can abuse food and medication to get attention. They are very self-deceptive and deny their motives and selfishness.
Level 8 - They are entitled. They believe that they can get anything they want from others.
Level 9 - They justify their behavior because they tell themselves they are abused and victimized by others. They are angry and bitter. They have a victim mentality and a 'woe is me' outlook on life. They are unwilling to take responsibility for their lack of happiness.

DEFENSE MECHANISM

The defense mechanism for the Two is repression. They will hide information about themselves from themselves. They do this to avoid experiencing painful emotions. They push their fears, needs, feelings, desires, etc., deep down inside in order to control them. Twos believe that if they are able to control these things, then feelings of pain can be avoided. Twos want to maintain a helpful image. Because of this, they won't let on that they have any needs themselves. Their self-worth is dependent upon gaining the approval of others. This can take the form of being overly nice and complimentary towards others, which can sometimes come off as superficial. Twos are known to manipulate through flattery if needed. They make others depend on them, but really, they genuinely want to make a real connection.

CHILDHOOD PATTERNS

The Two child is warm, caring, kind, and they really want to please others.

They believe that they have to earn love, attention, and praise, so they do their best to express themselves in loving and generous ways. Their superpower allows them to feel and know what other people are feeling. Twos know the emotions and needs of others intuitively. This ability allows the Two to provide what others need without them having to ask. Twos become obsessed and addicted to the grateful responses from others and want to seek these responses over and over again. When they feel unwanted or unloved, they lean into their superpower and may manipulate others into giving them the love, affection and appreciation, they desire.

Twos may test others to see how much they are loved. They read body language, expressions, and look for cues from their parents and other authority figures and role models to figure out how much they are loved, wanted, and valued. If they can't find the information they are searching for, they feel hurt, deflated, and rejected. They don't believe that they are lovable, kind, or selfless. Because of this, they are constantly overextending themselves to be these things. They learned early on how to manipulate others with hopes of hearing that they are wanted and loved.

TRIGGERS FOR CONFLICT

When Twos are triggered, they may become intense and openly express how they are feeling and what someone else did wrong in the situation. They may become passive-aggressive and manipulative or more demanding and controlling.

Conflict in Twos may be triggered by them being taken advantage of or feeling like they were taken for granted. If they feel unappreciated or unheard, they may sense their emotions rising. If a Two feels rejected, replaceable, or feels that they aren't wanted, they are likely to become triggered and express themselves.

A HOW-TO GUIDE FOR THE HELPING AND PEOPLE-PLEASING STUDENT

- Help them to understand that their worth is not based on love and appreciation.
- Don't take advantage of their desire to help.
- Two children really try their best to do the right thing all of the time. They want to make you proud.
- It's important to pay attention to their level of development:
  - A healthy Type Two is unselfish, humble, and understands the importance of taking care of themselves.
  - An average Type Two has a difficult time saying "no" and may sacrifice themselves in order to help someone else.
  - An unhealthy Type Two is entitled and self-serving and has a victim mentality. They place the blame on everyone else for their unhappiness.
- If a student is at a healthy level, encourage and reassure them that they are on the right path.
- If a student is at an unhealthy level, pay attention to their environment. What may be triggering their negative behaviors and attitudes? Find ways to work with their strengths and make them more confident.
- Pushing, nagging, or focusing on their mistakes and flaws will more than likely only make matters worse. If needed, seek professional help and guidance.

FAMOUS ENNEAGRAM TWOS

- Dolly Parton
- Jimmy Carter
- Maya Angelou
- Mother Teresa
- Stevie Wonder
- Jennifer Garner
- Mr. Rogers
- Anna (*Frozen*)

TYPE TWO QUESTIONNAIRE

Does the student:

☐ desire to be a great student so they are liked by their teachers?

☐ put other people's needs before their own?

☐ seem intuitive and know how other people are feeling or what other people need without being asked?

☐ have a strong sense of empathy?

☐ freely offer advice, their time, or help to others?

☐ get their feelings hurt more easily than other children?

☐ knowingly or unknowingly manipulate others to get what they want by offering them help and support?

☐ get called a teacher's pet?

☐ rarely ask for things they need or express what they need?

☐ seem to want to be with others more than anything else?

ADULT REFLECTIONS ON BEING A HELPING AND PEOPLE-PLEASING STUDENT

1. I was very self-motivated, and I was in the gifted and talented classes.
2. I feared letting people down who had high expectations for me.
3. I was a great student and athlete. I participated in practically everything.
4. People said that I was a teacher's pet.
5. I did not like homework, so sometimes I wouldn't do it. My overall average wasn't affected too much because I did well on everything else.
6. I was a huge people-pleaser and I made myself fit in with any group of people.
7. I was laid back and friendly. I was friends with the jocks and the nerds.
8. I was pretty insecure. I never felt like I was good enough.
9. I was capable of getting straight As, but I didn't apply myself. But everyone liked me!
10. I wanted to make my parents and teachers happy, so I was obsessed about getting good grades.

WHAT BEING A HELPING AND PEOPLE-PLEASING STUDENT WAS LIKE:

Middle school for me was tough socially because I was a pacifist and a pushover. I got bullied and pushed around. I was a decent student. I earned mostly Bs and Cs.

As high school progressed, I found myself caring way more about my interpersonal relationships than my schoolwork. Being the likable kid was way more important to me.

I was always a sweet, quiet kid who was scared to get in trouble, but somewhere around 7th grade, I started making little comments in class that made people laugh. That also made me a target for bullies. "He thinks he's SO funny," etc.

Kids would make fun of my clothes, shoes, haircut, pimply face, etc. I had a speech impediment, too, so it made it hard to hit back with witty comebacks. All of my friends just stayed quiet so as to not incur the wrath of the bully onto them, which made me sad in the moment, but I understand now.

It was somewhere around 9th grade where girls started to notice me and my sense of humor. I realized then that the things I was going to take with me the rest of my life were going to be my interactions with people. School stuff was important but relationships and how to deal with them was going to be more important.

- **Nicholas Flora, 2W3**

I mostly always enjoyed school. I was shy in my younger years, but I always had friends. As I got older, especially in high school, I was very social, and I always wanted to be a good student. As a matter of fact, my mom found me one day in elementary school creating my own test to study.

Teachers liked me. Overall, truly all of my years in school were fairly positive. Sure, I had those awkward middle school years, but basically, I liked school. People liked me and I liked most people. At my 5th grade and 8th grade graduations I was voted by my classmates and teachers for the Citizenship award. In hindsight my Type Two and One wing wanted to be nice and do the right thing. In high school I was involved in clubs, student government, and was on homecoming and spirit courts.

I was a hard-working student. As mentioned, I wanted to be good and please my teachers and my parents. As I went into high school, I was placed in honors and gifted classes but was not in fact gifted. I think the One wing of being a hard worker is what got me there. I made all As and Bs my entire life and only one C. Interestingly enough, I preferred to work alone rather than with friends on schoolwork because I felt like I did most of the work. On the other hand, I loved hanging out with friends after school.

As I look back, while I always enjoyed school, I did place a lot of pressure on myself. I remember often having stomach aches and headaches, but never told anyone. I would just keep going. I would never ask a teacher for help if I didn't understand something. Sometimes I would ask a friend, but never teachers.

As I mentioned, when I was young, I was very shy except with a couple of close friends and family. When I moved into middle and high school, I became much more outgoing. I was pretty much friends with everyone. I had my close group, but I talked to everyone and mostly everyone talked to me. Once I got my driver's license I was on the go! My grandfather used to say, "she has moved into her car."

- **Allison B., 2W1**

ENNEAGRAM TYPE THREE
The Popular & Engaging Student

*"Girl there ain't no I in 'team,'
but you know there is a 'me.'
And you can't spell 'awesome' without 'me.'
I promise that you'll never find another like me."*

- *Me*, Taylor Swift

energetic

optimistic

confident

superficial

deceptive

driven

ambitious

efficient

Enneagram Type Three

Type Threes are high achievers and want to be seen as such. They are willing to overcome any odds to be successful.

Because Threes focus on excellence and exemplary performance, they are an inspiration to those around them. They do not rely on exterior motives; they are internally motivated to achieve.

Type Threes thrive on accomplishment and have a strong desire to stand out as an example that others should follow. They are great goal setters and enjoy the completion of each task on their journey to meet and exceed their goals.

Type Threes are focused on excellence, in everything they do and in how they look. They are ambitious and are able to put how they feel aside if necessary.

For Type Threes, image is everything, which can sometimes cause them to "act" like everything is okay even if it isn't. They only want the world to see the successful parts of them, even if that means losing sight of who they truly are. They base their worth on their accomplishments, which means they are in a perpetual state of unfulfillment.

In healthy times, they are able to appreciate who they are and separate from their accomplishments. Their ambition and confidence are contagious, and others look to them for inspiration. Their natural ability and drive allow them to excel at a multitude of different things.

Threes know how to make a first impression and put their best foot forward. They know how to present themselves in ways that show off their confidence. They want to be liked and valued by others, so they strive to always be presentable.

IN A NUTSHELL...

The Three student is a performer. They are optimistic, flexible, and hold themselves to the highest standard in all that they do. They believe that their value is based on the things they accomplish; they believe that they are only as good as what they do.

Core Fear - Inadequacy, being worthless, failing to be successful; being incompetent
Core Desire - To be seen, to be successful, valuable, and admired
Focus - Looking the part. Achieving success.
Goal - To receive affirmation and praise from others. To be the best.

Biggest Struggle - Deceit

Threes are chameleons. They can become whoever they need to be to fit the crowd they are in. They believe that they are only as good as what they accomplish or how they present themselves to the world. Because of this, they will embellish the truth and shapeshift into the ideal image in any given situation. By doing this, everyone sees and admires them. But they may lose sight of who they truly are deep down, because the person they present themselves to be is not always the real them. During this process, not only do they deceive others, but themselves as well.

CHARACTERISTICS

Threes are competitive. Winning and being the best is important to them. While they are competitive, they can also be a team player. It depends on the stakes and the situation. They don't mind cutting corners if they can get the job done more quickly and efficiently.

Threes are charming and energetic. They are often in the popular crowd.

They are natural leaders and role models for younger students. They don't like to sit still; not because they are hyperactive (not ruling that out), but more because if they are still then they aren't moving, doing, or accomplishing. Threes are go-getters and they don't like when others slow them down.

Three students need to be admired and they need to be liked. This may cause them to go against their own morals, values, and wishes in order to be accepted into a specific clique. Threes are more likely to give in to peer pressure if they believe that it will benefit their image or reputation.

COMMUNICATION STYLE

Threes are high-achieving go-getters. They have high expectations of themselves in all areas. They are competitive and constantly push themselves to the next level, whatever that may be to them. They must be better than they were yesterday. They need others to see and recognize all of their accomplishments. It's not enough to just succeed, they need to be congratulated and appreciated for their hard work. Threes are positive and natural charmers when it comes to communicating. They know exactly what to say and when to say it.

They are motivating and seem to ask useful questions that help push them forward. Because they are achievement driven, they love to set goals and use words targeted towards the future: tomorrow, next week, next year, etc.

Below are a few suggestions on how to effectively communicate with a Popular and Engaging Student:

- It doesn't feel fake for Threes to adapt to different environments and shapeshift to fit in; it feels necessary.
- While they seem confident, they still need reassurance. Make sure their hard work is recognized.
- If they share about their personal life or their feelings with you, listen. They don't open up to just anyone.
- Make sure your directions are clear and direct.
- Feedback is appreciated because Threes always want to be better, but make sure the feedback is constructive. They take criticism personally.

LEARNING STYLE

Threes want to be the best. They want to outperform everyone else in the room. They compare themselves to the other students in the classroom to determine how much effort they need to put in in order to come out on top. They will definitely cut corners if it will get the assignment done more quickly and efficiently.

They prefer the directions to be clear and direct. If they are confused or unsure, they aren't going to be as efficient in completing the task or assignment because they will need to figure out what they need to do. They may ask a peer for more direction or their teacher directly. Either way, it will take them longer to complete the assignment and they don't like to be slowed down.

Threes are very concerned with how they present themselves to the world. Threes need to fit in, they need to be admired, and they need to achieve. If the classroom isn't their stage, they have one somewhere else, whether that's on a field or a court, or another extracurricular or hobby.

Threes may secretly compete with other members of their class to outperform them and be the best. However, they may also be in a higher-level class for the status and recognition that comes with it; this may cause them to work much harder than the other students just to keep up. They are capable and want to prove they belong. They enjoy theoretical lessons that are concise and to the point. They seek information that will lead them to getting results and achievement.

WORK ETHIC

Threes are the stand-out students. They are internally motivated and driven to be the best. They will find shortcuts and understand that things don't have to be perfect to be great.

If they think they can't do something well, they aren't likely to attempt it because they fear failure. But, if they do fail, they are able to spin it so it looks like success. Threes are your braggers and boasters. They love to show off and talk about their accomplishments. They love praise and attention. They are super competitive and sensitive to criticism.

Report card feedback may say: Student is a real asset to the classroom, student may give in to peer pressure, or student is self-motivated.

PREFERRED CLASSROOM ENVIRONMENT

Three students enjoy a classroom full of students who are competent and eager to learn. They are social and will chat with their classmates, but not to the detriment of missing key information. They don't want to set themselves back on their quest to be the best.

They need expectations to be clearly defined. As mentioned previously, Threes will cut corners. If they know exactly what is expected of them, they will figure out how to do it most efficiently, even if they have to bend the rules to do so.

They are sensitive to criticism, but they value feedback and opportunities for self-reflection. If they don't know what they did wrong, they don't know how to do better in the future. Give them feedback but give it to them constructively and gently.

Encourage Threes to track their personal progress. This will give them an opportunity to compete against themselves, rather than trying to compete with and be better than their classmates. Remind them that self-improvement is the goal, not winning.

WINGS

The wings attached to Type Three are The Helping and People-Pleasing Student (Type Two) and The Unique and Creative Student (Type Four). These wings can be abbreviated as 3W2 and 3W4.

THE 3W2

The Type Three with the Two wing tends to be warm, more encouraging, sociable, and popular. They enjoy being the center of attention and in the spotlight. When they are struggling, they are extremely competitive, insecure, and suffer from comparisonitis. This wing is inspiring because they are able to see how to make others feel seen and heard. They have the ability to make others feel special and supported.

THE 3W4

The Type Three with the Four wing tends to be more focused on work and success. They are introspective, sensitive, artistic, imaginative, and pretentious. When they are struggling, they are more afraid of failure and need to receive more praise for their accomplishments. This wing is inspiring because they are able to master a skill with creativity and introspection.

THINGS TO LEARN

Type Threes would benefit from learning that their accomplishments do not define their worth. They need to realize that they are loved for who they are, not what they achieve. They would benefit from knowing that it's okay to come in second place and to relax, enjoy the moment, and have fun. Threes are going to compete, it's who they are. As mentioned before, keep reminding them that the only person they truly need to compete with is themselves.

IN STRESS

In stress, a Three moves towards an average to an unhealthy Type Nine. They will become very disengaged and shut down. They may resist help when it is offered. When a Three is stressed, nothing is ever their fault. They place blame on everyone except themselves. They will stay busy in order to avoid looking lazy, but their busyness isn't necessarily productive. You may find that they want to be alone so they will withdraw and may become depressed. Threes will find a comforting activity or routine and 'numb out' to life to avoid reality.

IN GROWTH

In growth, a Three moves towards a healthy Type Six. They are comfortable with who they are and are able to separate themselves from their achievements. They are able to find peace in the things they accomplish. They are able to receive help from others and will use their gifts and talents with the intent of helping everyone, as opposed to only helping themselves. In growth, they become less competitive and more cooperative. Threes will be able to accept and love who they are and won't need to change or shapeshift in order to fit in.

LEVELS OF DEVELOPMENT

Healthy levels:

Level 1 - (at their best) They are authentic. They portray themselves to be exactly who they are. They are giving and modest. They fully accept themselves. They are gentle and kind.
Level 2 - They are energetic. They have high self-esteem and are confident and competent. They fully believe in themselves and their abilities. They easily adapt to situations. They are charming and likable.
Level 3 - They strive to continue self-improvement. They reflect on how to be the best version of themselves. They are admired and highly effective. They are very motivating and inspiring. Others want to be like them.

Average levels:
Level 4 - They constantly worry about their progress. They give themselves value based on their achievement. They play the comparison game in academics, social status, and success. They fear failure. They need to be the best.
Level 5 - They are worried about their self-image and are concerned with how they are perceived by others. They set expectations for themselves based on others' opinions. They are efficient, but at the detriment of losing sight of who they are. They can become superficial and fake.
Level 6 - They live to impress others with their status. They practice self-promotion and exaggerate to make themselves sound and appear better than what they are. They have a 'look at me' attitude and always want to be in the spotlight. Deep down they are jealous of the success of others, but they use arrogance as a defense mechanism. They hide their jealously and highlight and embellish their achievements.

Unhealthy levels:

Level 7 - They fear failure and being humiliated. They will expose the flaws or mistakes of others for their own benefit. They are opportunistic and are jealous of the success of others. They will do whatever it takes to save the image or illusion they have created for themselves.
Level 8 - They are sneaky, manipulative, and deceptive. They can't allow their mistakes to be exposed. They will betray others in order to rise above them. They can't be trusted and could sabotage the success of others for their own personal gain.
Level 9 - They can become obsessed with destroying the happiness of others. They can't handle their failures and they become vindictive. They can demonstrate psychopathic behaviors. They can be narcissistic.

DEFENSE MECHANISM

The defense mechanism for the Three is identification. Threes use identification to avoid the fear of being rejected. They embody the traits in others that they respect and admire and shape-shift instead of being their true and authentic selves. They do this to maintain their self-image of being successful. Identification is stepping into and playing a role so well that you lose sight of who you are authentically. The pressure to maintain a successful and admirable image prevents the Three from recognizing their own needs and feelings. Threes find it challenging to be themselves and let go of the role-playing since they get praise and attention from a world that values and affirms achievement. They want to completely embody the traits and qualities that they feel others admire so they will be admired, too.

CHILDHOOD PATTERNS

The Three child has the understanding that emotions or self-care are unimportant, and the most important thing is to be accomplished and successful. The Three child is taught that their acceptance and love is based on their accomplishments, which keeps them in a perpetual state of ambition and the desire to achieve. Somewhere they got the idea that they are only loved when they achieve. If they are praised when they bring home a 100% on a test or score a goal at their soccer game, something about that praise strikes a chord. If they achieve, they feel love. So, they continue to achieve in order to feel loved. If the preferred image does not come naturally to them, they mold themselves to fit whatever image that may be. They absolutely must be the best and be liked by everyone.

The Three child knows who they need to connect with in order to gain acceptance. Needing constant recognition to feel accepted and loved, the Three child will often exaggerate and embellish the truth if it means they will be more admired by their peers. The Three child is insanely competitive and equates their worth with their achievements.

TRIGGERS FOR CONFLICT

When Threes are triggered, they may lose sight of their relationships with others and focus their attention on achievement. They may begin to work harder and speak more sharply and in quick, short sentences in order to be more efficient and productive. Threes don't want to be slowed down, but when they are triggered, they like it even less.

Conflict in Threes may be triggered by being blamed for someone else's mistake, bad judgment, work, performance, or actions. Another trigger for a Three is getting humiliated or embarrassed. Threes always want to look the part and be successful. Their self-image and reputation is everything to them. If they have accomplished something and don't receive praise or recognition, that will most likely cause them to feel triggered. Purposefully setting them up to fail or putting them in a position where failure is a high possibility is a way to possibly set them off.

A HOW-TO GUIDE FOR THE POPULAR AND ENGAGING STUDENT

- Encourage your Three students to realize that they only need to be better than the person they were yesterday. They don't need to compete with anyone else.
- Help them to understand that being honest with themselves will get them further than embellishing the truth or inflating their importance.
- Three children love the spotlight. Highlight their work and praise them publicly when it's appropriate.
- It's important to pay attention to their level of development:
    - A healthy Type Three is self-accepting and authentic. They motivate others and are interested in self-improvement.
    - An average Type Three is obsessed with their performance. They are image-conscious and deeply desire to impress others at all costs.
    - An unhealthy Type Three fears failure and humiliation. They are devious and may try to ruin the happiness of others.
    - If a student is at a healthy level, encourage and reassure them that they are on the right path.
- If a student is at an unhealthy level, pay attention to their environment. What may be triggering their negative behaviors and attitudes? Find ways to work with their strengths and make them more confident.
- Pushing, nagging, or focusing on their mistakes and flaws will more than likely only make matters worse. If needed, seek professional help and guidance.

FAMOUS ENNEAGRAM THREES

- Taylor Swift
- Tony Robbins
- Muhammed Ali
- Tom Cruise
- David Copperfield
- Dwayne Johnson
- Oprah Winfrey
- Lightning McQueen (*Cars*)

TYPE THREE QUESTIONNAIRE

Does the student:

☐ want to complete tasks successfully?

☐ easily adapt to different social situations in order to fit in and make friends?

☐ have good self-esteem?

☐ like to keep a clean and organized space?

☐ enjoy the spotlight and want to be the center of attention?

☐ boast about their accomplishments and show off to others?

☐ appear to be confident and optimistic?

☐ have many different interests?

☐ want to be the best in every activity they participate in?

☐ take pride in their appearance?

ADULT REFLECTIONS ON BEING A POPULAR AND ENGAGING STUDENT

1. I cried when I got my first B.
2. I loved when my teachers wrote notes or put stickers on my work.
3. I followed people like Tony Robbins on social media.
4. I was an all-A student and I secretly competed with the other all A students in my grade.
5. I got bored and distracted easily if I wasn't challenged.
6. I wanted to have positive relationships with my teachers and the kids in my class. I really loved going to school every day.
7. I was a cheerleader, and everyone loved me. I was voted Homecoming Queen.
8. I was always on the go. If I wasn't busy with sports, I would hang out with my friends.
9. I wanted to be at the top of my class. I took all honors and AP classes.
10. I was involved in a lot of different clubs, and I was the class president. I was voted most likely to succeed.

WHAT BEING A POPULAR AND ENGAGING STUDENT WAS LIKE:

I vividly remember arguing with my teacher in the middle of a test. The whole class was quiet and sitting there taking the test. We were arguing back and forth because I didn't know the answer and I was outraged that she would put something on the test that I didn't know. I always knew the answers, how was there something on this test that I didn't know? I thought she was wrong. I thought she had made a mistake on the test.

Growing up I had an older sister, and I privately decided that I needed to compete with her. Because she was older, I felt like I needed to earn my space or my own spot in the world. My parents didn't demand that I get good grades, I took that upon myself. A 98% wasn't good enough, I had to have a 100%. I wanted to be best friends with my teachers, and I wanted them to know me by name.

I competed with other people, girls specifically, that were at the top of my class and usually I was best friends with them. We were neck in neck all of the time and we all tried to be the best. One of my friends specifically, we competed against each other from 4th grade through senior year. We are still really good friends to this day.

I was the kid that teachers wanted to have in their classroom. I always wanted praise and validation, so I kept performing and doing the things I needed to do to receive that.

- **Marta Spirk, 3W2**

When I was a kid, everything was about the here-and-now. I can still hear my mom's voice at 7 am when I shook her out of her slumber, with pen in hand, saying "Mom, can you sign my report card?" Her response was one I heard many times in my life: "Does it have to be NOW?!" In my mind, everything had to be now. Everyone was way too slow, everyone slept too long, and everyone took way too long to do things.

I remember coming home from school and immediately starting on homework. But it wasn't because I loved homework, it was because homework was an impediment to my fun, and the sooner I got it out of the way, the sooner I could play. I loved games and sports, I loved anything to do with art and music, and I loved laughing, usually at the expense of others with practical jokes.

I consistently had the same work ethic throughout middle school and high school - to study hard and get the best grades I possibly could in every class. I listened intently, took thorough notes, asked questions when I didn't understand the material, and prioritized homework, making sure to get it done as quickly as possible upon returning home from school. I couldn't focus for long periods of time (and still can't), as I find it mentally draining.

There were definite problem area subjects, in particular the sciences, like chemistry and physics. The teachers I had were obviously very knowledgeable but weren't able to make a connection with me. One physics teacher I had basically had his back turned toward the class the entire lesson writing notes on the blackboard, while every now and then muttering some explanation of the material. Classes like that made me discouraged because I wanted to learn, but the teachers offered no encouragement to learn because they were so disconnected.

I was the proverbial class clown and would do anything to get a laugh from my classmates. I imitated voices and sounds really well, incessantly mocked my teachers' quirky voices, and even mimicked the sound of the bell so I could end class early. Silly, of course, but I was successful at it. So much so that I got my entire classes to pick up their belongings and leave early. But one day my French teacher caught me in mid-impersonation, with my mouth in the shape of a giant 'O', and said angrily, "La cloche sonne dans ta tête!" meaning: "The bell is ringing in your head!"

In social groups, I was very friendly. I found myself doing more listening than talking. I paid attention to people when they spoke, always made sure to keep good eye contact, and ask questions so I stayed engaged. I preferred not to talk about myself unless I got the sense that people really wanted to hear what I had to say. I read non-verbal cues really well and can immediately pick up when a person is interested in me or not. If the interest is there, I love to talk and tell people about myself, especially the things that interest me! But when I get the sense that people aren't interested in what I have to say, I'll immediately shut down and get quiet.

I performed far better in classes where the teacher was personable, approachable, and able to connect with me. In my junior year of high school, there was a push to get into the best college possible. The school I went to pushed students very hard in this direction, as did my mom, and this made me very motivated to do even better in school because I wanted to get into the most prestigious college.

I took the SAT that year and put a lot of time into prepping for the test, getting out study aids, and doing practice tests. I scored an 1100 on the SAT, and I remember I was very disappointed with the result. I compared myself with my friends and fellow classmates, and when I heard that some of them scored over 1200, it made me even more motivated to try harder; so, I took the test again the following year. When I improved by only 10 points, I was greatly disappointed because I had set a goal to get a score of 1200 or more. I remember getting into the comparison game thinking, "how could my friend who's such a slacker have scored 1200? I'm smarter than him!"

I was always an ambitious and motivated student. Getting good grades was paramount to anything else and comparing myself to my friends and classmates fueled my motivation to perform better even more.

- **Peter Sarfati, 3W2**

As a student, I was responsible and curious. I appreciated good teaching, organized materials, and clear expectations from my teachers. I did have to work harder than others, though. Learning was not effortless for me unless it was something that I was passionate about. I occasionally had late homework or missed assignments, and I allowed my other interests to distract me.

I constantly tried to stay on top of all of my responsibilities and reassure myself that I was successful. I was always producing some sort of art or music in the midst of my academic responsibilities and my after-school job. I struggled with feeling like a failure if I didn't handle my stress perfectly.

I loved to attend parties and sporting events. I had a great group of creative friends and we made up stories and wrote songs when we got together. I was involved in leading music with my youth group at my church. I often needed time alone to balance all of the ambitious goals I wanted to achieve.

- **male, 3W4**

ENNEAGRAM TYPE FOUR
The Creative & Unique Student

*"Look out cause here I come.
And I'm marching on to the beat I drum.
I'm not scared to be seen, I make no apologies.
This is me."*

- *This Is Me*, The Greatest Showman

creative

refined

warm

temperamental

possessive

self-aware

intuitive

passionate

Enneagram Type Four

Fours, at their best, are intuitive, sensual, creative, insightful, and desire to express themselves. At their worst, they can be moody, selfish, and overly-dramatic. Fours desire to be seen as individuals that stand out among others. They are willing to be open about how they are feeling and about their compassion for others. They desire every experience to be meaningful and unique. Fours see the beauty in life.

Fours enjoy using their creativity to express themselves. They desire honest and authentic connections with others, despite their self-conscious nature. Fours tend to dwell on the past and frequently compare their present circumstances to their ideal circumstances.

Fours feel very deeply, which can manifest into feeling distant from others. When Fours are able to process and express their deep emotions in a healthy way, they are able to meaningfully impact and care for those around them.

They have the ability to feel and love deeply, and they have a unique ability to understand the world around them. They are not afraid to experience deep and/or painful emotions.

Fours desire a meaningful existence in this world through experiences and relationships. They allow comparison to take up too much space in their head, whether that's comparing themselves to other people, ruminating over the past, or feeling like life isn't meeting their expectations.

Focusing on themselves can result in an increased sense of self and can result in them becoming emotionally exhausting and self-absorbed. The ability to control their emotions serves them very well and allows them to deeply connect with others in a beautiful and unique way.

IN A NUTSHELL...

The Four student is a dreamer. They are creative, unique, intuitive, and warm. They are able to put words to emotions and situations that others may not be able to express. They want to be true to themselves and they want others to be real and authentic, too. They can almost instantly spot when someone isn't acting genuinely. They can sense who they can trust, who is a genuine person, and who isn't. They can't stand people who are fake or try to be someone they aren't. Most of all, Fours want to be unique and stand out. They want to be their own person and will point out all of the ways that they are different.

Core Fear - Being inadequate, plain, mundane, or emotionally cut off
Core Desire - Being unique, special, and authentic
Focus - What is wrong with me?
Goal - Be true to themselves and make their mark.

Biggest Struggle - Envy

Fours typically feel that they are extremely flawed and that something tremendous inside of them is missing. They believe that others have the qualities that they lack. They believe that others are able to get the things that they want.

CHARACTERISTICS

Fours want to be authentic. They want to be known for their hearts; for who they are. They are creative, even if they don't recognize that skill in themselves. Fours want to stand out from the crowd. They want to present themselves as different, special, and unique, but they also want to belong. Fours care a great deal about beauty and they look for the beauty in people, places, and things. Some Fours may express themselves through their choice of clothes. Others may write poetry, journal, or draw. If they aren't artistically talented, they may find beauty in music or nature.

Fours are sensitive and can be temperamental and moody. They are able to experience a large range of emotions that other types can't. They set high expectations for people, events, situations, conversations, etc., and feel frustrated when reality doesn't quite match what they imagined.

They want to be liked and they want to fit in, but they never completely feel like they do. The most popular Four may still feel like an outsider in their own group.

COMMUNICATION STYLE

Fours can be known for being dramatic. They can almost romanticize small issues and make them seem larger than life. They definitely seek deep and meaningful conversation with others, as long as it's authentic and genuine. Fours can tell when someone isn't being genuine or honest with them.

Fours aren't afraid to get personal and vulnerable and share their story or their truth. In turn, they want others to be vulnerable with them. If you have a student who shares personal information with you, or a student who openly shares details about their personal lives with their classmates, there is a chance that they are a Four. This isn't attention seeking behavior, it's them showing up as who they are and being raw and honest about it.

Fours want to be validated. Let them know that you hear them and you understand what they are saying.

Below are a few suggestions on how to effectively communicate with a Unique and Creative Student:

- Sometimes they don't want to share details if they are too personal or too hard to explain.
- They always feel like something is missing or lacking in them. If they are skilled at something, or they do something well, let them know. They may not recognize their gifts and talents.
- Mirror their feelings. If they are excited about something, get excited with them. If you don't, they may feel like they are too intense and withdraw or feel like you aren't interested.
- Acknowledge their feelings, regardless of what happened to cause them. Their truth and perspective is valid.
- Pay attention. Fours really appreciate when you remember details or stories that they share with you.

LEARNING STYLE

Similarly to Twos, Fours desire a personal or an emotional connection to the topic or lesson. They will grasp a concept much more easily if it connects to them in some way, shape, or form. Not only will they better understand the lesson, but they will be more motivated to understand the lesson if they feel a personal or emotional connection to the material.

Fours will try their best when they are motivated. They will study when they need to, and they will perform well when they need to, or if they want to. If they don't feel that something is important, they will do enough to just
complete the task at hand. They will most likely procrastinate to complete it, too. To put it simply, Fours need to be inspired.

If something is important to them, or meaningful, they will work extremely hard and give their best effort. An idea for Fours is to give choices in the classroom to assess for the same skill. If they have an opportunity to choose their project or assignment, they are more likely to find connection to the task and complete it well.

Something to remember with Fours, they do their best work when inspiration sets in. This is one reason why they procrastinate; they are waiting for the right mood to kick in so they can produce their best work.

WORK ETHIC

Fours are sensitive to criticism; even constructive criticism can throw them off. They do not want to disappoint you or do the wrong thing. If they have worked hard on something and they receive negative feedback, they may withdraw.

They challenge themselves to be different, to be unique and extraordinary. They don't want to complete the same project thateveryone else is doing. They want to create something special.

Fours want to be different, but they also want to fit in and belong. They want to stand out, but they don't want to stand out at the same time. If they realize that they are engaging or acting differently from the other students in class, they may become self-conscious. They really struggle with comparing themselves to others. They don't want to be like or act like everyone else. They really do want to be different and unique but have this internal conflict between wanting to be different and wanting to fit in at the same time.

Report card feedback may say: Student contributes personal experiences that relate to group discussions, student can be dramatic or overly emotional, or student is honest and trustworthy.

PREFERRED CLASSROOM ENVIRONMENT

Four students want a comfortable and aesthetically pleasing environment. Their quality of work is highly affected by their mood. If they are in a "boring" classroom, they may not be up for giving their best effort. If they aren't inspired, their work may suffer.

They need to express themselves and process their emotions. Fours feel things deeply and they hold on to them until they are resolved. Some Fours may sit with issues even after they are resolved. If there was an argument with a parent or friend that morning or the night before, the Four may have an off day. They may or may not tell you what happened, but if you notice that something is off, ask them if they are okay. Give them space if they need it and practice patience with them.

Fours love to put their unique spin on things. They want to be different. The more they are able to choose or personalize their assignments, the better. This will motivate them which will create space for them to demonstrate their knowledge. Sometimes project guidelines are limiting and can hold students back from producing their best work.

Fours don't have to be the best or the smartest kid in the class, but they want to be the most authentic. Feeling like they don't fit in is quite common. Because of this, sometimes Fours will adjust the rules or guidelines to fit their needs and desires.

WINGS

The wings attached to Type Four are The Popular and Engaging Student (Type Three) and The Observant and Intelligent Student (Type Five). These wings can be abbreviated as 4W3 and 4W5.

THE 4W3

The Type Four with the Three wing tends to be more extroverted, upbeat, ambitious, emotionally volatile, concerned with image, and flamboyant. When they are struggling, they are much more concerned with what others think of them and their emotions can fluctuate. This wing is inspiring because they are determined to make their own special mark on the world with their ambition and authenticity.

THE 4W5

The Type Four with the Five wing tends to be more introverted, intellectual, withdrawn, reserved, observant, depressed, and have intellectual depth. When they are struggling, they are more withdrawn and consumed with their emotions. They strongly desire independence. This wing is inspiring because they are able to combine their intellect with their emotions to produce incredible work.

THINGS TO LEARN

Fours would benefit from learning to be objective and to focus on the positives. It's also helpful for them to realize that they don't necessarily have to act on their emotions. They can process and feel their emotions, but their feelings shouldn't drive their behavior. They need to learn that constructive criticism is supposed to be helpful; it's not a personal attack.

IN STRESS

In stress, a Four moves towards an average to an unhealthy Type Two. They can become clingy and needy in their relationships with others and start to use manipulation tactics to get what they need from others. They may become possessive in relationships by not wanting their friends or loved ones to spend time with anyone else. When their feelings are hurt, they may withdraw from others and remove themselves from the situation.

IN GROWTH

In growth, a Four moves towards a healthy Type One. They become less impulsive and have more control over their emotions. They are able to be more grounded, objective, and practical. These Fours are able to relax and completely accept and love themselves for who they are. They become more invested in helping others and contributing to things bigger than themselves. They are able to tackle the mundane, day-to-day things about life with a sense of pride and recognize these 'boring' tasks as opportunities to become more responsible, organized, and helpful to others.

LEVELS OF DEVELOPMENT

Healthy levels:

Level 1 - (at their best) They are supremely creative and can shape every experience into something valuable and then share that value with others.
Level 2 - They are self-aware and very sensitive to their feelings. Intuitive with themselves and others. They are compassionate and gentle. They have a strong sense of feeling and demonstrate impulse control.
Level 3 - They are completely true to themselves. These Fours are authentic, real, vulnerable, and honest with themselves. They can be serious or funny. They are strong emotionally and have a deep sense of who they are.

Average levels:

Level 4 - They believe that the world is a beautiful, artistic, and romantic place to be. They are able to form strong and valuable relationships. They sometimes live through fantasy and their imagination. They feel strongly and can be emotional.
Level 5 - They take everything personally. They are introverted and shy around others. They can be very self-conscious and self-absorbed. They protect themselves by withdrawing from social situations. They can't deal with spontaneity, and they withdraw and take time away from others to sort through their feelings.
Level 6 - They feel that they are different from everyone else which leads them to believe they can do things differently without consequence. They are dreamers and live in a world of fantasy. The rules don't apply to them. They can have self-pity and become jealous of others. This leads to self-indulgence and becoming more and more unproductive.

Unhealthy levels:

Level 7 - They become angry and depressed when they fail. They become withdrawn and block out their emotions. They are extremely tired and are sometimes unable to carry out their day-to-day tasks.
Level 8 - Their thoughts are tormented, and they can begin to hate themselves. They blame others for their failures and push everyone away.

<u>Level 9 -</u> They feel completely hopeless and may turn to drug and alcohol abuse to escape their pain. In extreme cases, they can have an emotional breakdown or begin to hurt themselves. They can become avoidant and depressed.

DEFENSE MECHANISM

The defense mechanism for the Four is introjection. Fours use introjection to help them cope with painful information and maintain an authentic self-image. Introjection is absorbing and internalizing any negative information into the idea of who you are. Fours tune out the positive things said about them and absorb the negative. They would rather create their own pain. Introjection causes the Four to inflict pain on themselves, which in turn, takes away the opportunity for others to inflict pain on them. This takes away the opportunity for others to reject or criticize them. Fours don't respond to criticism from others; they take the words and internalize them. Fours tend to blame themselves for the things that go wrong around them. If they reject themselves first, then they can't be rejected.

CHILDHOOD PATTERNS

Fours often feel different from their parents, siblings, and those around them. They do not see themselves reflected in one or both of their parents or guardians. This causes them to feel disconnected and misunderstood. Feeling misunderstood and different causes them to experience feelings of abandonment and loneliness. They do not feel that their parents or guardians take an interest in knowing them completely or even trying to understand them. This causes them to feel rejected, like there is something fundamentally missing and flawed about them.

Since Fours cannot see themselves in their parents or guardians, they turn inward to find their authentic self. They desire to show the world how unique and special they are. Discovering and understanding the depths of themselves is their most important goal.

They regularly focus on this missing piece and wonder how things could be different if they had this thing that everyone else has. They constantly compare themselves to others and adults should refrain from asking a Four why they can't be more like so and so.

TRIGGERS FOR CONFLICT

When Fours are triggered, either they are going to shut down and withdraw or bluntly voice their feelings and opinions. They won't be able to move forward unless they understand the whole process or situation, including how they feel about it and the purpose or bigger meaning behind it. Fours regularly feel misunderstood; if they are triggered or struggling, they are going to be adamant that you understand their perspective, their truth, and how they feel. They will explain themselves over and over again until you 'get it.' They may hold onto their feelings and hold a grudge for a while. If they are in a state where they want to stay in their mood, it's best to not even try to cheer them up. They will move on when they are ready.

Conflict in Fours may be triggered by peer pressure or being asked to do something that goes against who they authentically are. They desire to be special, different, unique, and authentic; if they feel that they aren't seen, heard, or valued then they may shut down. If they are accused of being fake or phony, they may get defensive and list all of the ways that they are genuine and authentic. They also struggle with envy. If they find themselves in a situation where the envy starts to creep to the surface, they may become triggered.

A HOW-TO GUIDE FOR THE UNIQUE AND CREATIVE STUDENT

- When possible, give the Four student a choice. When they are able to decide how to demonstrate their knowledge, their work will improve.
- Be gentle with criticism and feedback. Fours can take things to heart and a simple "fix this" could result in the student withdrawing and shutting down. This could hinder their learning.
- Four children want to be special. If they have created an extraordinary project or did really great on an assignment, praise them and put their work on display.
- It's important to pay attention to their level of development:
  - A healthy Type Four is able to find something beautiful and valuable in every experience. They are self-aware and gentle.
  - An average Type Four can live in their imagination and take things personally. They may go the extra mile to show others that they are different and unique.
  - An unhealthy Type Four can become angry when they fail and blame their failures on others. They push others away.
- If a student is at a healthy level, encourage and reassure them that they are on the right path.
- If a student is at an unhealthy level, pay attention to their environment. What may be triggering their negative behaviors and attitudes? Find ways to work with their strengths and make them more confident.
- Pushing, nagging, or focusing on their mistakes and flaws will more than likely only make matters worse. If needed, seek professional help and guidance.

FAMOUS ENNEAGRAM FOURS

- Jackie Kennedy Onassis
- Bob Dylan
- Prince Charles
- Johnny Depp
- Kate Winslet
- Dakota Fanning
- Gene Wilder
- Belle (*Beauty and The Beast*)

TYPE FOUR QUESTIONNAIRE

Does the student:

feel left out or feel like they don't fit in?

feel like there is something different or unique about them?

enjoy being creative?

seem to be more sensitive and get their feelings hurt more easily than others?

feel like they are misunderstood and always need to explain what they mean?

wish they had things that others have?

feel the need to be different or special and stand out from the crowd?

experience a wide range of emotions?

feel comfortable in a melancholy state and seem to not want to be cheered up at times?

seem to have a push/pull relationship, where they push you away and then pull you back in?

ADULT REFLECTIONS ON BEING A UNIQUE AND CREATIVE STUDENT

1. I caught myself daydreaming a lot, especially if I didn't think the class was important or if I was bored.
2. I was pretty emotional, and people always used to tell me that I was dramatic.
3. I tried to slide under the radar and go unnoticed by my teachers.
4. I wanted to fit in with the popular kids, but they never fully accepted me. I was captain of the cheer squad, but I still didn't get invited places.
5. I spent most of my time with my boyfriend.
6. I was very scatterbrained, and I was always running late.
7. I chose to take lower-level classes so that I could maintain a good GPA instead of taking higher-level classes that would have challenged and pushed me. I was comfortable being the smart kid in the average classes.
8. I was really shy (still am) until you got to know me, but once I came out of my shell I wouldn't stop talking. I used to get in trouble a lot in school for talking.
9. I was really smart and capable, but I didn't apply myself because I thought school was a waste of time.
10. I loved to write poems about how I was feeling and about things that were going on in my life. I also had an online journal.

WHAT BEING A UNIQUE AND CREATIVE STUDENT WAS LIKE:

I was "good" at being a student, but I always felt like something was missing, or that something just wasn't quite right.

I understood the importance of school and having good grades at an early age. I chased straight As, being congratulated for having the highest grades in class, and being told I was intelligent and that I had a bright future ahead.

My parents never had to push me to do well because I did that all on my own. In fact, my mom often had to teach me how to take pressure off of myself (even in elementary school) and would even beg me to stay home from school for mental breaks.

While school seemed to consume me, I often battled with the question, "What do you want to be when you grow up?" I would always respond with, "pediatrician," because I was always told I would make an exceptional doctor. This is what I thought my "bright future" was supposed to look like.

While I had a plan to become a doctor, I often found myself daydreaming about being a singer/songwriter, an actress, and/or an author. I didn't see those as actual careers because I was told I needed to become a doctor, so I buried the temptation and kept making my grades my number one priority. Nevertheless, this tango between my creative and ambitious side continued into high school.

On the surface, I was considered an exceptional student. I made straight As, I was in the National Honor Society, Beta Club and I was the secretary in Health Occupation Students of America. Behind closed doors, I was writing songs, practicing my dance routines (I was a competitive cheerleader) in the mirror (pretending I was performing for an audience), starting blogs, building websites, and writing short stories I published online.

Socially, I felt super awkward. I felt invisible, but at the same time, I was always paranoid that the other kids were talking about me. Big friend groups weren't really my thing. I usually had 1-2 best friends that I kept super close, because anything more always made me feel uncomfortable and paranoid.

Because of this, I hated being called on, or raising my hand in class. It didn't take long for me to develop a fear of public speaking. If I knew I had to speak in front of class, I would panic about it for weeks, and would often try to stay home from school just to get out of presenting.

While I was "good" at being a student, I was incredibly lost. I let my worthiness be defined by my grades and didn't follow my creative instinct until I was older. It was no wonder I always felt like something was missing - it was.

- **Hannah Brindley, 4W3**

I was the talkative student. Each school year and each time that progress reports and report cards were sent home, I'd have the same remark "constantly talking in class." That was me. I never denied it but my parents certainly did their best parenting to try and curve it, but it didn't work. I was also the student in high school who took full advantage of us not having to wear uniforms, so I wore what I wanted, which most of the time it ended me up in the office for a dress code violation. I would either be sent home to change or told I couldn't wear it again. Knowing me, I would.

I was the high school student who strived to learn all I could outside of the classroom. I wasn't into extracurricular activities or looking to be the star of this team or that team, I wanted to work. After school, I went to my part time retail job. My written reports were always thorough because I did the research. I hated working in groups; I always preferred to work alone. My mother raised my siblings and I to know that a good reader is a good speller and a good person to have conversation with. I'd read the newspaper; it wouldn't matter to me as long as I was reading and able to write.

Overall, I enjoyed school. I had a good number of friends, many of which I'm still close to today. If you asked me if I would like to go back to high school, I'd emphatically say "No." I'm happy to have graduated and be done.

My social life was normal. When I wasn't working, I would hang out with friends at the movies, I'd talk on the phone, or do other regular teenage kid things. I wasn't looking to be a part of social clubs or athletics; it just wasn't my thing.

- **Jeanna Byrd, 4W5**

I always did well in school academically. I typically had high grades and enjoyed the sense of achievement I got from being successful. For me, school was mostly easy, and I could get by without having to work hard or study.

Throughout all of my school years, I found that I related pretty well with adults, commonly hearing that I was "wise beyond my years." This didn't necessarily translate into my relationships with peers, though. In my early school years, I was bullied a lot and I always felt misunderstood. People treated me as if I was 'too much.' I felt that I could not find friends that accepted me or my interests.

Because of that, in high school I changed who I was. I made myself more "acceptable." This led to popularity and relationships, but I always felt dissatisfied, hoping to find the perfect friends or the perfect girlfriend. I constantly pushed people away and then pulled them back in again, all while feeling unloved for who I was. I had a lot of friends, and I was well-liked, but I felt so alone.

It took me years to accept myself, love myself and my interests, and understand that I could find stability in my relationships with others. I still have many fond memories, but I wish I had someone who could have guided me through all of the intense emotions I experienced as a child and teen and tell me that I was enough and not too much. I wish someone had told me that they loved me for exactly who I was.

- **Eric Muñoz, Jr, 4W3**

ENNEAGRAM TYPE FIVE
The Observant & Intelligent Student

*"All day, starin' at the ceilin' makin'
friends with shadows on my wall.
All night, hearing voices tellin' me
that I should get some sleep because
tomorrow might be good for something."*

- *Unwell*, Matchbox Twenty

wise

curious

innovative

private

detached

independent

collected

insightful

Enneagram Type Five

Fives are rational and logical thinkers. They would rather work by themselves than with a team. Fives are fiercely independent, perceptive, and curious. Because Fives prefer to be alone, they can be viewed as distant, eccentric, and difficult to understand. Their analytical skills make them excellent visionaries for the future.

Fives are very private and prefer to observe rather than engage with others. Full of knowledge and highly intelligent, Fives reserve their attention and focus for thinking about and learning new things.

Fives are assets during a crisis because they are able to remain detached from their emotions. They thrive in environments where they are able to make their own decisions without oversight.

They are experts at compartmentalizing and are often perceived as socially awkward, eccentric, or anti-social. When they are put into social situations, they tend to keep to themselves and may need time alone after to decompress and recharge.

Sometimes the world can be an intrusive and overwhelming place.

Because of this, Fives focus their attention on protecting their energy.

Their protective boundaries can be interpreted as emotional distance and avoidance by others. If Fives feel that they do not have enough knowledge or insight into something, they are less likely to engage and might even retreat further into their own minds.

They fear being vulnerable with others which can impede their ability to make authentic connections with them. Often the requirements of human connections seem outside of their abilities, which will cause them to continue to create distance from relationships and interactions with others. Finding balance will mean that they are able to give more of themselves and interact more from their hearts.

IN A NUTSHELL...

The Five student is a deep thinker. They are logical, analytical, and have a deep desire to understand and be competent. They are the kids who will take something apart just to see how it works. They can feel like the world is too overwhelming and will drift into their mind and imagination where things make more sense. Their mind is their retreat and, oftentimes, their inner world is much more real than their outer world.

Fives love to learn and they love to solve problems. Because of this, they will sit with a problem until it is solved or until they realize that information is missing and the problem is not solvable.

Core Fear - Being unprepared or incompetent, being incapable
Core Desire - Being intelligent, competent, and capable
Focus - To be prepared and do everything well.
Goal - Eliminate distractions in order to study and learn.

Biggest Struggle - Greed

Fives typically feel that they lack the resources they need and that too much interaction with others will completely use up all of their stored energy. Because of this, they limit themselves from contact with others and minimize their needs. Imagine a cell phone battery; the other eight types wake up with a ninety to one hundred percent charged battery, Fives wake up with a battery life of about seventy to eighty percent. Because of this, they limit their resources and social interactions because they tire much more easily.

CHARACTERISTICS

Fives are insightful and they don't mind being alone. In fact, many times they prefer to be alone. They wish that others would understand that their desire to be alone isn't personal, it's just what they need sometimes. Fives are very private people and they don't share a lot of information about themselves. They are introverted and observant. They are independent and are able to take care of themselves. You can give a Five student a set of directions and leave them alone for the rest of the class.

Fives are very curious. They love to learn and when they find a subject they are interested in, they want to know everything about that subject. When Fives are focused or in the zone, they can completely lose track of time, forget to eat, miss phone calls or texts, or become oblivious to things going on around them. If they are working independently in the library, it wouldn't be far-stretched to say that they may not hear the bell and then show up late to their next class.

Fives really enjoy being around like-minded people. When they find someone whose interests and intellect match theirs, they can become super sociable and talkative.

COMMUNICATION STYLE

For the most part, Fives are quiet. They are factual and logical. When they have conversations, they want them to be to the point and focused on the topic at hand. Fives are typically emotionally detached. So they aren't going to bring emotions into a conversation and they aren't going to make a decision based on how they feel.

Fives like to process and understand completely before engaging in conversation. If they are being quiet, it's not because they are ignoring you. It's likely because they want to make sure they know exactly what they are talking about before they speak.

Below are a few suggestions on how to effectively communicate with an Observant and Intelligent Student:

- They want to understand your perspective, even if they don't agree. They want you to reciprocate.
- They do have feelings even if they don't show or talk about them.
- Don't pressure them to participate or engage. They really are quite comfortable watching.
- If they express how they feel, don't make a big deal about it. If you

make a joke or a comment about them finally talking, they may not feel comfortable expressing themselves to you again.

LEARNING STYLE

Five students love to learn, but they aren't okay with teachers or other authority figures who don't appear to know what they are talking about. Fives may find themselves judging the knowledge level of their teachers and mentors.

Fives do not like to be unprepared or put on the spot. Their biggest fear is to appear ignorant or incompetent. If you call on them to respond (without advance notice) and they aren't completely sure of the answer or have any significant input to give, that could cause them to shut down.

They love to observe and watch how things work before trying them out t hemselves. They learn best through observation. They also prefer to fully understand something before working with or talking to others about the topic.

Fives prefer to work alone. This helps them maintain their privacy, protect their energy, and respect their boundaries. If they are working on a group project, make sure you give them some time alone before the class is over so they can regroup and prepare for the rest of their day.

Fives enjoy self-reflection. They feel like there is always something to learn and that they can never fully master a subject. When they are given the opportunity to reflect on their learning, they are able to make sense and process what they are learning and figure out what they need to do next to fully understand the topic.

WORK ETHIC

When Fives are interested, they want to learn all there is to know about a topic. They don't necessarily want to have the highest grade or make all As in school, but they do want to dive in and understand everything about a topic that sparks their curiosity. They get frustrated when they are interrupted if they are zoned in and focused on something.

Fives don't want to start on something until they know exactly what they are doing. They will observe and study details until they feel confident enough to begin. When they find a topic of interest, by the end of the semester or the year, they may be able to teach their teacher a thing or two.

School can seem quite boring or under stimulating for Fives. For the most part, they will get decent grades, but they don't put pressure on themselves to be the best or the smartest kid in the classroom. Additionally, they are much more interested and invested in the topics that they want to learn about. Sometimes, that doesn't match up with the actual curriculum.

Report card feedback may say: Student spends time completing independent studies on classroom topics that have sparked interest, student regularly spends time alone, or student provides insightful comments during whole group discussion.

PREFERRED CLASSROOM ENVIRONMENT

Five students desire to learn. They love an environment that encourages curiosity and learning. They love intellectual discussions and exploring topics of interest in depth.

Fives need to be given time to really dive into research and explore the content of the lesson, especially if they are interested in what's being taught. What to make a Five student's day? If you notice that they are really into the topic, send them to the library to do their own research and have them report back to you about what they learned. This gives them independence and a chance to study the material the way they want to.

Fives love peace and quiet. They love to be by themselves. Noisy classrooms are a distraction and can be draining for a Five. The same goes with group work. Fives much prefer to work on their own. Forced socialization is not something a Five enjoys.

School can be tough for a Five because they really do love to learn, but the social aspect and expectations can be challenging. Fives tend to have a love-hate relationship with school.

WINGS

The wings attached to Type Five are The Unique and Creative Student (Type Four) and The Questioning and Loyal Student (Type Six). These wings can be abbreviated as 5W4 and 5W6.

THE 5W4

The Type Five with the Four wing tends to be more withdrawn, isolated, creative, and emotional. When they are struggling, they are much more sensitive than people realize. They tend to detach and create distance between themselves and others. This wing is inspiring because they are able to dissect problems and pull things apart in order to look at them from a different perspective.

THE 5W6

The Type Five with the Six wing tends to be more intellectual and observant and is a great problem-solver. When they are struggling, they find that their relationships with others take a turn. They may live in their mind more than usual. This wing is inspiring because they are able to sit with a problem until it's solved. They thrive on researching and analyzing problems and find power from intellect.

THINGS TO LEARN

Fives would benefit from learning to relax and have fun. They are comfortable watching what's going on around them instead of participating but getting out of their comfort zone and joining in can be a good thing. They can learn to start speaking out more and realizing that sometimes they have to make a move. Thinking about something isn't going to get the job done. It's also important for Fives to learn that they really are valued for who they are and that it's okay for them to have needs and express them.

IN STRESS

In stress, a Five moves towards an average to an unhealthy Type Seven. They can become scattered and demonstrate hyperactivity. They may become chatty and impulsive. In stress, Fives may take on more than they can handle and not give themselves enough time to really learn something before moving on to the next project or jumping into something else. They can become impatient, cynical, and jaded.

IN GROWTH

In growth, a Five moves towards a healthy Type Eight. They become more decisive. They aren't as withdrawn or uncomfortable in social situations or group settings. Fives in growth are more connected to their emotions, are more confident in their abilities and knowledge, and are eager to take action. They are able to trust their instincts.

LEVELS OF DEVELOPMENT

Healthy levels:

Level 1 - (at their best) They are open-minded. They are visionaries and see things in their true light, for what and who they are. They make discoveries and create new ways of thinking and doing
Level 2 - They are very observant. They have incredible insight. They are curious, intelligent, and focused. There is nothing that they overlook. They have intense concentration and give 100 percent focus to something that catches their eye.
Level 3 - They are able to acquire whatever skill set that interests them. They love to learn and become excited to learn more about a topic of interest. They are experts. They are innovative, inventive, original, and incredibly valuable. They are very independent.

Average levels:

Level 4 - They don't act until they fully understand. Everything needs to be worked out in their mind, first. They prepare, practice, and prepare some more. They are very studious. They often become specialized in a certain field.
Level 5 - They become super detached when they get deep into an idea or a fantasy. They get lost in their visions rather than deal with reality. They can be intrigued by dark subjects and topics with disturbing content. They can be high-strung and intense.
Level 6 - They grow cynical and can be very argumentative. They think they are always correct and can have extreme beliefs. They view things negatively and can be fairly antagonistic.

Unhealthy levels:

Level 7 - They isolate themselves from reality. They are unstable and fearful. They reject others and social situations. They become reclusive.
Level 8 - They can become obsessed, to the point of becoming frightened,

with gross, dark, and disturbing ideas and content.

Level 9 - A psychotic breakdown is possible. They are deranged and self-destructive. They could have personality disorders such as Schizophrenia.

DEFENSE MECHANISM

The defense mechanism for the Five is isolation. Fives use isolation in order to avoid feeling overwhelmed and empty, as well as to keep a knowledgeable self-image. Fives isolate and distance themselves by escaping into their minds and detaching themselves from their emotions. Isolating allows them to stay inside their comfort zone and protect their energy and resources. Isolation may also be demonstrated by physically withdrawing from others. They believe that this is a healthy way to cope, but in reality, this negatively affects their relationships with the people in their life.

CHILDHOOD PATTERNS

Being social does not come naturally for a Five child. They often do not feel secure in their relationship with their parents or in their interactions with others, so they focus on their love of learning. The outside world is overwhelming, so they are desperate to create their own private space outside of the oversight and scrutiny of their parents or guardians. Time alone allows the Five child space to sort out their emotions, thoughts and feelings.

The Five child may take apart their toys to see how every piece works. To them, knowledge is the key to being accepted so they spend their effort learning new things, observing the world, and asking a lot of questions. They cherish their alone time which is where a Five child feels most comfortable and secure. In the privacy of their own space, the Five child can sort through complex emotions and restore the energy that was depleted throughout the day. The Five child probably enjoys collecting things and working with technology.

TRIGGERS FOR CONFLICT

When Fives are triggered, they can use their intellect to belittle others and may come across as being arrogant. They will likely detach from their emotions in order to observe what is going on around them. Depending on the environment and situation, they may then physically retreat, withdraw, and isolate to a safe space in order to process their feelings alone.

Conflict in Fives may be triggered by being given a task or an assignment that seems overwhelming. If a person close to them has broken their trust by sharing something confidential or has been dishonest with them, they will most likely withdraw from that individual. Fives need time alone to recharge; if they don't get that time, they can become triggered. They also don't like to be surprised, intruded upon, or feel obligated to do something.

A HOW-TO GUIDE FOR THE OBSERVANT AND INTELLIGENT STUDENT

- When possible, give the Five student time alone to recharge. When they are able to have a little bit of time to themselves, they can better prepare for the next class. This is especially important on days when the task involves group work.
- Fives withdraw when they need to recharge or when they feel incompetent.
- They do not want to be put on the spot to answer a question, especially if they don't know the answer.
- Five children want to learn. School can be a difficult place because being social doesn't come naturally to them.
- It's important to pay attention to their level of development:
    - A healthy Type Five is open minded and observant. They are innovative and independent.
    - An average Type Five won't participate or act on something unless they are confident in their abilities and knowledge. They can be cynical and argumentative.
    - An unhealthy Type Five will withdraw and isolate themselves from reality. They reject others and can become obsessed with dark ideas and thoughts.
- If a student is at a healthy level, encourage and reassure them that they are on the right path.
- If a student is at an unhealthy level, pay attention to their environment. What may be triggering their negative behaviors and attitudes? Find ways to work with their strengths and make them more confident.
- Pushing, nagging, or focusing on their mistakes and flaws will more than likely only make matters worse. If needed, seek professional help and guidance.

FAMOUS ENNEAGRAM FIVES

- Bill Gates
- Jane Goodall
- Tim Burton
- Amelia Earhart
- Diane Sawyer
- Albert Einstein
- Mark Zuckerberg
- Albus Dumbledore (*Harry Potter*)

TYPE FIVE QUESTIONNAIRE

Does the student:

☐ have a shy personality?

☐ regularly seek time alone?

☐ prefer to stand back and watch, instead of participate?

☐ tire easily in social situations?

☐ seem to not care about social norms or struggle to understand social behaviors?

☐ tend to avoid large gatherings and social situations?

☐ enjoy taking things apart to see how they work?

☐ enjoy asking questions and learning about new topics?

☐ like their privacy and struggle when people ask them personal questions or give them too much attention?

☐ prefer to play alone than with a friend or a group of friends?

ADULT REFLECTIONS ON BEING AN OBSERVANT AND INTELLIGENT STUDENT

1. I received decent grades in subjects like history, English, and psychology, but I had to work really hard. I couldn't cram the night before a test because it wasn't about just learning the topic, I had to understand the topic and its connections to other things.
2. I was a wall flower and had nerdy interests. I got mostly Bs, and I had friends who were very similar to me. I enjoyed school, even though I was one who preferred to just watch from the sidelines (while reading a book). I also liked to do things with computers and technology.
3. I was an outsider, but I had a hunger for knowledge. Even though I was a pretty good student, I was always on the edge of boredom.
4. I loved the learning part of school, and I got better at the social aspect. I preferred to learn and explore what I found to be interesting versus what was being taught.
5. I was really awkward and shy, and I had zero fashion sense. I literally wore the same outfit every day: a pair of jeans, a t-shirt, and my converse sneakers.
6. I was always a straight A student, but I also challenged my teachers at times.
7. I was the girl who never talked. I had a hard time making friends and got made fun or a lot for being quiet. I had a lot of anxiety about going to school every day. I was miserable and would cry most mornings. I pretended to be sick a lot, but sometimes I really got sick, physically, from the anxiety.
8. In high school I was the outsider. I loved hard rock and heavy metal music and I went to church every Sunday. I loved my history and government classes and any class that was related to current events.
9. I was really good at the school portion. I got straight As, but I really found the material boring. I always looked for ways to get creative with my projects and make them visually appealing so I could have some enjoyment.
10. I made decent grades, but that was just an attempt to go unnoticed. I didn't want to be the best, but I also didn't want to fail in any area and therefore stand out.

WHAT BEING AN OBSERVANT AND INTELLIGENT STUDENT WAS LIKE:

Middle and high school were pretty easy, academically. I pretty much flew under the radar and got As and Bs. I was extremely quiet in class, and I never asked for help or raised my hand. If I didn't understand something I'd try my best to figure it out on my own, ask a friend, and then ask the teacher for help (this was rare). The two classes (world history and chemistry) I struggled in, I was perfectly fine getting a C. I was a master at procrastination, and this actually never bit me in the butt.

Socially, I had multiple different groups of friends - band nerds/smart kids, athletes, and friends I grew up with in my neighborhood. I was a bit of a chameleon. I was in band and jazz band through 9th grade, and I gave this up so I could play more sports. I was an athlete and played varsity golf, varsity lacrosse, and basketball throughout high school. I was the captain of my golf and lacrosse team for multiple years. I must have really leaned into integrating to my Eight.

With all of that I was still extremely quiet and an observer. I always had way more information about others than they did about me. Sports were a place I was extremely competent in, so I really leaned into them. It was also a great place for friendships because there was a set purpose, we were all there for. Being socially anxious, this provided an in for me.

- **Chantille Rees, 5W6**

I was probably the only kid in high school at the pool with Rene Descartes' Discourse on Method and the latest issue of Cosmo. I was not afraid to walk into the teacher's lounge and steal their doughnuts or put some vodka in my water bottle. I often corrected my teachers, and one time I was asked to leave the classroom over it.

I had this false, naïve presumption that I was in school to actually learn, and I was annoyed that nobody else was on board with that. I can quote one teacher, word for word, in her description of me. "There's no telling that kid." Once I knew something, you couldn't convince me I didn't know it. I didn't trust teachers to understand the material. I hated lectures. I just wanted to read the book and take the test. I hated waiting for the class to catch up to me. If I didn't understand something, I wanted the privacy to learn it on my own.

I remember I asked my Geometry teacher the ungodly question, "Why?" He responded, "Never ask why in math." I believe I wanted to know why all the angles in a triangle equal 180 degrees. God eventually showed me in a dream: just unwind all the angles in a triangle, and you get a straight line.

I expected to be treated like an adult. My issue I think was that I knew I was smarter than most adults, as most adults didn't take Calculus. I felt like if you can't do my homework, then who are you to tell me what to do? My father was the only person who could put me in my place with that, "I'm the guy who owns the car you drive."

I was socially awkward, not that I felt awkward socializing as I'd talk to anyone, but that my social skills were so bad that it made everyone in the room feel awkward. My dad often said, "Let me do the talking," because nobody knew what would fly out of my mouth. I still had friends, and my relationships with those people were vital to my success with grades, not the actual learning or being smart part.

One time in Physics we had a Take-Home-Final. It was ONE question, but one that required you to do about 50 different calculations. Something about a fake planet in outer space with a bunch of information about it. I remember diving in and realizing he didn't give me the gravity or force for the planet. So, I asked him in class, and he swore all the info I needed was on the final. I spent a week trying to figure it out, assuming I was missing something, and I couldn't. I needed that stinking number so bad. So, I bugged the class again, several times, the teacher swearing I had all the info I needed. The classroom eventually got annoyed, and the entire class asked me to shut up about it. They all implied I was some kind of idiot because they could figure out the question.

Out of desperation, I got on my Prodigy Internet at home, and I found some random email addresses to random math Professors at Harvard and Oxford. I emailed them my dilemma. A professor from Oxford emailed me back, God Bless his soul, and he agreed I needed a number for the planet's gravity. So he suggested I figure the calculations several ways to at least show that I can do the work and know the process. Several weeks later, the teacher finally told us our grades, and he explained that only two students passed the final. He apologized for forgetting to tell us the gravity of the planet and handed us our papers; I got a 100.

- **Michelle Grewe, 5W4**

I was an only child and the outside world felt really unnecessary. I was fairly outgoing and fearless, but I was pretty self-contained. I felt like I could never really connect enough with my classmates. I was ostracized and I had difficulty learning, so I stayed in my own little space and kept to myself. I would jump into conversations here and there, when I felt like I could contribute. I feverishly tried to fit in and intellectually prove myself, which I didn't really, because it wasn't coming from a confident place.

Around 7th or 8th grade I gained some popularity by becoming the class clown, but I was more laughed at than laughed with. It was better than nothing in my eyes. I would cling to the most powerful people in the school. I would make myself useful to them and which gave me some assurance.

I would say that I was rejected a lot from kindergarten through 8th grade. I didn't really have any sophistication and I wasn't well groomed. I think that's what my peers wanted. I didn't really have any friends that I would have over or hang out with outside of school. I had one friend who didn't go to my school who was very socially sophisticated; he was sort of like my life vest. I would hang out with him and then I'd go back to school.

As far as academics go, I was a poor student. If I didn't immediately understand something, I would give up. Persistence wasn't in my vocabulary, and I felt really discouraged by the whole academic process. A key set of emotions I'd contribute to my school age years are: loneliness, repetition, anxiety, fear, want, obnoxiousness.

As a whole, I didn't really feel like I was prepared at all. Everything was overwhelming. There wasn't a space safe enough. I was sensitive. I very much wanted to be a part of something and be someone. Be the thing that only people could determine me to be, but it didn't occur to me that I could self-determine who I was.

- **male, 5W4**

ENNEAGRAM TYPE SIX
The Questioning & Loyal Student

"When the sun shines, we'll shine together.
Told you I'll be here forever.
Said I'll always be your friend,
took an oath, I'ma stick it out 'til the end."

- Umbrella, Rihanna

likable

loyal

trustworthy

defensive

unpredictable

witty

responsible

practical

Enneagram Type Six

When Sixes are at their best, they are dependable, personable, organized, and they really enjoy using their sense of humor. But when they are at their worst, Sixes can be cynical, cautious, and overly suspicious of others.

Sixes desire to belong. They see themselves as dependable and they want others to see them as dependable and responsible, too, but sometimes their cautious nature can cause others to see them as wishy-washy, flaky, or fickle.

Sixes prefer to be a part of the group and they hope to have someone they trust take the leadership role. They don't want to be in a leadership position because they fear that being that role will open them up to unwanted criticism.

Sixes want to connect with people who are as trustworthy and responsible as they are, which means that it takes them longer to fully rely on someone. They may even create situations for the other person to prove themselves as trustworthy.

They tend to overthink situations and frequently consider the worst-case scenario in order to be more prepared. The motto of the Sixes is 'prepare for the worst, hope for the best.' Sixes will do well when they stop considering 'what if' and learn how to trust in themselves and their own decision-making skills.

They are constantly burdened by uncertainty and desire to be in control of any situation that could threaten them or someone they care about. They consistently rehearse in their minds what could go wrong and constantly ask themselves, 'what if.' This perpetual state of worry can be debilitating for Sixes and result in an inability to make decisions.

They are so overly cautious that it can unfairly burden their relationships because they can misplace fear and distrust. But at their healthiest, they are able to overcome their fear, find peace, and trust themselves.

IN A NUTSHELL...

The Six student is loyal and committed. They prefer certainty, predictability, consistency, and comfort. They like clear rules, regulations, procedures, and boundaries. They recognize what is safe and what is maybe not so safe. When Sixes join a club or a team, they stick it out. A minor disagreement or argument won't cause them to quit. Being benched won't cause them to quit. They made a commitment; they are going to see it through.

They question themselves constantly. They really struggle to make a decision and lean on trusted friends, family, and other experts for advice because they don't trust their own thought process or ability to make decisions.

Sixes may frequently deal with stomach aches or headaches that stem from anxiety over asking for some extra help or guidance or needing the directions to be clarified in front of the rest of the class. They desperately want support and guidance, but they don't always feel comfortable asking for it.

Core Fear - Not having guidance, not being supported or secure, not being safe
Core Desire - To have certainty, support, guidance, and security; to be safe
Focus - All of the things that could go wrong.
Goal - Find a trusted authority figure or role model to learn from and look up to.

Biggest Struggle - Fear

Sixes typically check out their surroundings in order to predict and prevent bad things from happening, especially worst-case scenarios. This causes them to live in a perpetual state of worry and regularly experience anxiety.

CHARACTERISTICS

Sixes are dependable, reliable, committed, trustworthy, anxious, rebellious, and defensive.

Sixes learn to worry early on in life. They learn that the world isn't safe, and they realize that the adults in their lives can't always be trusted to do the right thing or to keep them safe. This causes them to either obey or rebel.

There are two types of Sixes - phobic Sixes and counterphobic Sixes. Phobic Sixes obey the rules and aim to please. They believe that authority figures are their security net, so they want to be loyal and give their best. They are the most fearful out of the nine types. Their fear can be paralyzing. Counterphobic Sixes aren't so keen on authority figures and they don't always trust those in leadership positions or authority roles. This causes them to rebel or be less compliant than a phobic Six. Counterphobic Sixes can feel as though someone always has a hidden agenda or an ulterior motive. These Sixes overcome their fears by facing them head on rather than falling victim to them, unlike phobic Sixes. Most Sixes are a healthy combination of phobic and counterphobic.

Sixes can resemble Ones. They can appear organized, responsible, and perfectionistic. The difference between the Six and the One is that the Six is trying to calm their anxieties by making their outer world as predictable as possible, and the One is trying to calm their 'inner critic' by always doing the right thing.

COMMUNICATION STYLE

Sixes can see both sides to most situations and typically will question the other or play devil's advocate. This helps them to feel confident and more secure. The more questions they ask or the more perspectives they are able to see, the more they understand what is going on, which leads to feeling safe and secure.

Sixes choose their words carefully. They don't want to come back to a conversation later with what they meant to say or apologize for something they didn't mean to say.

Sixes don't typically enjoy public speaking or class presentations. The thought of being the only person at the front of the classroom giving a presentation can give them anxiety.

Below are a few suggestions on how to effectively communicate with a Questioning and Loyal Student:

- Give them as much information as possible. The less they know, the more they think, which can lead to worst case scenarios.
- If Sixes are doing well, praise them. They will internalize a lack of praise as not being liked and believe that they are being targeted.
- If a Six makes a good decision, tell them. It will help them improve their confidence in making decisions.
- They aren't asking questions to challenge you; they truly just want to make sure they completely understand.
- Be truthful with Sixes. They don't want part of the truth; they want the whole truth.

LEARNING STYLE

Six students need structure. They need routine. They need predictability. Sixes thrive when they know what to expect, but they can panic when life throws them a curveball. If your classroom expectations, rules, and procedures are the same day in and day out, a Six will feel very comfortable.

If you know you are going to have a substitute ahead of time, letting your class know that you will be out will give your Six students time to mentally prepare. If they walk into an unexpected change, they may begin to feel anxious which could cause them to act out, shut down, or feel sick.

Rules and procedures need to make sense. Sixes tend to question authority and if they don't understand a rule or procedure, they are likely to question it. If you have a rule that says, "throw all of your trash away at the end of class," a type Six may ask "why?" or "but what if I have to blow my nose? Do I just leave the tissue on my desk?" Making your classroom rules and procedures simple and reasonable will help your Six students.

Counterphobic Sixes will ask questions until they completely understand what is expected of them. Phobic Sixes may be too afraid to ask a question in front of anyone, so make sure you make yourself available for students to ask questions privately or frequently check in with students while they are working to make sure they are on the right track.

Sixes desire reassurance and support. When they get positive feedback, it helps them learn that they are able to trust themselves and that they are doing things correctly. Sixes over-analyze and struggle to trust their abilities.

WORK ETHIC

Sixes want to understand what they are supposed to do, and they also want to understand the teacher. I've mentioned this before, but Sixes are very wary of authority figures. They aren't sure who to trust, who to listen to, or who to follow. They can be very skeptical which leads them to ask a lot of questions. Sixes aren't trying to challenge you with their questions, they are trying to make sure they fully understand.

Like the Five students, Sixes want to watch first. They are much more comfortable if they have the opportunity to observe before doing a task on their own.

Sixes tend to procrastinate and over-analyze. Not only do they lack trust in authority, but they lack trust in themselves. For the most part, they want to do a great job and they want to please.

Some Sixes may become frustrated if their work is not correct the first time. They may struggle with the planning and research phase. Help Sixes overcome their tendency to procrastinate by encouraging them to get started right away, even if they only do a little bit at a time.

Report card feedback may say: Student double and triple checks work carefully before submitting it, student does not easily adjust to change, or student is able to plan and carry out group activities effectively.

PREFERRED CLASSROOM ENVIRONMENT

Six students want their peers and classmates to be responsible for their actions and their education. They want their classmates to come to class prepared and ready to learn. Sixes are very loyal and committed; this makes them excellent team players and ideal partners for group assignments.

They enjoy open-ended classroom discussion. Six students have a lot of questions, and they want to make sure they are in a safe and welcoming place to ask them and get the answers they need.

Sixes struggle with anxiety, more so than any other Enneagram type. This can cause them to get frequent stomach aches or headaches at school, request to stay home from school or become emotional or aggressive about going to school, experience shyness, or struggle in testing environments.

To help alleviate some of their anxieties, and support their need for security and safety, teachers could create a sense of predictability, introduce change gradually, and provide specific instructions, routines, and guidelines. Six students desire community. They want to be a part of something: a team, a club, a group, etc. They fear being alone or being abandoned. They struggle to trust themselves. Having a social support system around them makes them feel more comfortable and confident.

WINGS

The wings attached to Type Six are The Observant and Intelligent Student (Type Five) and The High-Energy and Adventurous Student (Type Seven). These wings can be abbreviated as 6W5 and 6W7.

THE 6W5

The Type Six with the Five wing tends to be more organized, perceptive, knowledgeable, and withdrawn. They are more self-controlled, responsible, and ethical. They are intense and speak their mind. This wing can be mistyped as a One or look like an Eight. When they are struggling, they are more suspicious of others and isolate themselves. This wing is inspiring because they are a voice for the underdogs. The 6W5 will go to bat for the underdog and stand up to defend them.

THE 6W7

The Type Six with the Seven wing tends to be wittier, engaging, sociable, friendly, and supportive. When they are struggling, they can become anxious and hard-working, but they also tend to procrastinate. They can be more reactive and feel pressure internally become anxious and hard-working, but they also tend to procrastinate. They can be more reactive and feel pressure internally to make quick decisions. This wing is inspiring because they are very warm and thoughtful people. They constantly look out for problems that could arise, but they want to have fun, too.

THINGS TO LEARN

Sixes would benefit from learning to trust and believe in themselves. They want to be certain of every outcome and they love predictability, but life isn't always certain or predictable. Learning to trust that they are capable of making a good decision and doing the right thing will help them become more confident in making future decisions. They can help to ease their anxieties by facing their insecurities head on and realizing that everything will be okay. Sometimes, the scariest things are the things worth doing.

IN STRESS

In stress, a Six moves towards an average to an unhealthy Type Three. They can demonstrate workaholic tendencies and worry about what others think of them. They may refuse to try something new if they feel that they won't succeed. They may strategize ways to charm and form alliances with others who will help keep them safe and secure. They may become arrogant and think that they are the only ones who can possibly see all sides and every possible outcome. In order to avoid feeling anxious, a stressed Six will stay incredibly busy and on the go.

IN GROWTH

In growth, a Six moves towards a healthy Type Nine. They give themselves time to relax and allow their minds to slow down. They are able to empathize and become more compassionate with others. A Six in growth becomes more confident in their ability to make decisions and they are able to reassure others, instead of being the one who needs constant reassurance. They are able to trust themselves and are more peaceful emotionally.

LEVELS OF DEVELOPMENT

Healthy levels:

Level 1 - (at their best) They fully trust themselves and others. They are independent and self-affirming. They believe in themselves and are courageous. They are leaders and positive thinkers.
Level 2 - They can bring about strong emotional responses from others. They are appealing and lovable. They build trust and bond well with others. They are able to form strong relationships.
Level 3 - They are dedicated to people and causes that they truly believe in. They are responsible and trustworthy. They sacrifice for others and create stability and security in their lives and the lives of others.

Average levels:

Level 4 - They invest their time and energy in things that they believe will keep them safe. They look to peers and authority for security and stability. They constantly anticipate problems and issues.
Level 5 - Passive-aggressiveness can pop up if they feel overwhelmed with tasks to complete. They begin to procrastinate and have a hard time making decisions. They become negative and reactive and begin to send out mixed signals. They suffer from internal conflicts which cause them to be unpredictable. They can become anxious.
Level 6 - Sarcasm is their defense mechanism. They use it for battle when they are feeling insecure. They blame others for their problems and become very defensive. They can turn friends into enemies.

Unhealthy levels:

Level 7 - When they feel that they've lost their stability and security, they become panicky and feel defenseless. They look for a new or stronger authority figure to help fix their problems. They are divisive and can attack or berate others.
Level 8 - They believe that everyone is out to get them. They act irrationally and lash out to their peers and authority figures. This could possibly result in the things they fear (lack of support and security, violence) coming to life.
Level 9 - They become self-destructive and hysterical. They can turn to drugs and alcohol to escape. They can become extremely passive-aggressive and could turn to self-harm.

DEFENSE MECHANISM

The defense mechanism for the Six is projection. Sixes use projection to avoid their own issues and maintain a self-image of being hard-working and committed. Projection is when someone unconsciously attributes their emotions, thoughts, behaviors, characteristics, motives, etc. onto someone else, both positive and negative. The more they project, the more they create a false reality. Sixes are more likely to project when they are feeling anxious. Positive feelings are projected in order to assure safety, security, and loyalty in their relationships with others and authority figures. Negative feelings are projected onto others as a way to justify their own inner feelings of fear, worry, and lack of trust. Because their projections are their reality, this can ultimately create conflict with others.

CHILDHOOD PATTERNS

Six children desire support, guidance, and security because they feel that the world is a dangerous place. Six children take warnings like "don't swallow your gum because it takes seven years to digest" or "don't swallow watermelon seeds or you'll grow one in your belly" seriously. They desperately want to avoid any potential harm or danger. At some point in their childhood, they learned that the adults in charge didn't always know what to do or couldn't always be trusted.

Many, but not all, Six children have unstable home lives. Their environments are shaky, causing them to doubt themselves and look to others for courage, support, and advice.

Their 'inner committee' starts at an early age and informs them of all of the things that could go wrong. They know every possible outcome so they can ensure safety. These voices cause confusion and create uncertainty and self-doubt.

Sixes seek guidance and security from trusted authority figures. They frequently ask for advice from those they trust before making a decision. Most of all, they want to feel safe and secure.

TRIGGERS FOR CONFLICT

When Sixes are triggered, they can either withdraw or become emotionally reactive. They may project their motives, thoughts, and feelings onto others because they believe that their projections are their current reality. Sixes tend to over-analyze in a regular environment; when they are triggered their over-analyzing nature can become intensified.

Conflict in Sixes may be triggered if they feel that they are being blamed, accused, or targeted. They may become triggered if someone isn't being genuine and honest with them or when others aren't as loyal and committed as they are. They don't want to be lied to or abandoned. Sixes may feel triggered if they are put under too much pressure or if others don't take their concerns and worries seriously.

A HOW-TO GUIDE FOR THE QUESTIONING AND LOYAL STUDENT

- When possible, give the Six student a heads up if an unexpected change or transition is coming. Predictability and certainty help them feel safe.
- Sixes can seem both shy and overly fearful or aggressive and fearless. This depends on whether they are phobic Sixes or counterphobic Sixes. All in all, though, every Six wants to feel safe and secure.
- Six students can be a challenge to figure out. Outwardly, they may appear as though nothing is bothering them, but they could be really anxious and fearful on the inside.
- It's important to pay attention to their level of development:
    - A healthy Type Six is able to form close relationships with others and completely trust themselves.
    - An average Type Six procrastinates and has a difficult time making decisions. They can also be passive-aggressive.
    - An unhealthy Type Six believes that everyone is out to get them.
- If a student is at a healthy level, encourage and reassure them that they are on the right path.
- If a student is at an unhealthy level, pay attention to their environment. What may be triggering their negative behaviors and attitudes? Find ways to work with their strengths and make them more confident.
- Pushing, nagging, or focusing on their mistakes and flaws will more than likely only make matters worse. If needed, seek professional help and guidance.

FAMOUS ENNEAGRAM SIXES

- Ellen DeGeneres
- Richard Nixon
- Sarah Jessica Parker
- David Letterman
- Tom Hanks
- Marilyn Monroe
- Prince Harry
- Mulan (*Mulan*)

TYPE SIX QUESTIONNAIRE

Does the student:

seem to worry more than most children?

desire to be safe and secure?

argue, just for the sake of arguing the opposing side?

ask a lot of questions?

have an over-active mind and constantly imagine worst-case scenarios?

seek advice from others in order to make a decision?

sometimes react in unpredictable ways that may seem extreme?

frequently change moods?

entertain, please, or help others in order to be liked?

feel like they always mess things up?

ADULT REFLECTIONS ON BEING A QUESTIONING AND LOYAL STUDENT

1. I was very, very shy in school until I discovered my Seven wing.
2. I was bullied a lot. I finally dropped out in high school.
3. I played devil's advocate in my classes about anything and everything that I could.
4. I did well in the classes that I liked, but if I didn't like my teacher, I wouldn't do my homework or participate in class unless it was to add a sarcastic comment here and there.
5. If I cared about a particular class, I would ace it. But if I didn't care about it or I didn't need it in order to graduate, I didn't put forth much effort.
6. I enjoyed school and I got along with all of my teachers. I always got good grades and enjoyed learning.
7. I was under confident and scared to answer a question or not know the answer to a question. I worked really hard to appear smarter than what I actually was.
8. I wanted to get attention from my teacher... but at the same time, I hated getting attention from my teacher.
9. I loved school but I was a bit of a bully.
10. I was pretty immature and tried to be the class clown.

WHAT BEING A QUESTIONING AND LOYAL STUDENT WAS LIKE:

I'm the oldest of six children, but I'm the only Enneagram Six. Growing up, I always loved to theorize how we all came from the same parents, we all grew up under the same rules, and we all attended the same types of schools, but we could all be described as different types of students.

My parents placed very little pressure on me to earn all As because I placed that pressure on myself. I was overly organized. The details of an assignment were something I would never overlook. In some ways, I was a teacher's dream. But I also stayed up until 2 am on multiple occasions to study just a little bit more, to rewrite the rules to the board game project I'd created, or to reread a part of the class novel I knew I wanted to talk about in class the next day. Unfortunately, I never felt like any of the work I produced was good enough. I always had a thousand questions along the way, but I was usually too nervous to ask for clarification from my teachers. Instead, I'd worry. Even if I'd over-prepared to show off my project or bring up an interesting piece of text, my anxiety - my self-doubt - kept me quiet more often than not.

A lot of this worry turned into stomach aches, especially when I was younger. My poor mother was called at least once (if not twice) a week to come pick me up from school because my tummy hurt. Looking back, I remember that there really was an ache happening, but I also remember that even then I knew it probably wasn't worthy of a phone call home. Looking back, I recognize that I was just an anxious perfectionist who was too scared to ask for the support I needed. The pressure I placed on myself to make everything I did the best was an impossible goal, so I must have always thought of myself as failing in some way. I think I felt like I was also letting my teachers down, because I knew they wanted me to do my best, and I wanted to please them.

It helped when I was given positive feedback, of course, and I remember feeling not so uptight when teachers voluntarily looked over my progress or made me feel okay about having a hard time getting started on an overwhelming task. My parents worked really hard to build up my confidence, and by the time I was in high school, I was able to more easily ask questions, share my ideas, and generally speak up in class. If it weren't for my parents helping me learn to advocate for myself, however, I'm not sure if I'd have ever gotten to that point.

Building on that lack of self-confidence, I always wanted to have better relationships with my teachers and peers in almost every single class

I've ever taken. Other students - students who didn't try as hard as I did - were able to joke around with the teacher and each other, and it seemed like there were so many fun friendships happening around me that I could never break into. I was too focused on following the rules and second guessing myself to enter into the banter. Part of me felt that this really wasn't fair because I was always doing what the teachers wanted me to do!

This introversion led me to usually have just one or two close friends. However, that, plus my self-doubt and my need to be perfect, made group work intensely difficult. What would I do if I had two best friends, but we could only have one partner? My entire week could be a mess of anxiety if I was left out. How embarrassing! The teacher assigns the groups, and I'm with someone I know is smarter than me; good luck getting me to speak up, take a chance, or really even learn something as I retreated into my hole of feeling that my best wasn't worth it. An assigned group where I was the de facto leader; I wouldn't say anything, but I'd do the work of five people in hopes that I'd both earn a perfect grade and maybe a new friend. Basically, me and group work had a love/hate relationship. Any chance to be with my classmates was one I wanted to enjoy, but it usually ended up being overwhelming and draining.

Because of all of this, I loved when everyone worked independently. As long as the teacher would come around and offer guidance without me necessarily having to raise my hand, I was in my happy place. I could focus on the details, recharge, check and recheck my work, and follow my own process to get to an end result that I could possibly be proud of.

- **Kirstin Boyd, 6W5**

I didn't particularly enjoy school. Doing schoolwork, studying for tests, taking tests; none of it was fun. I made decent grades which was nice, but I didn't feel like I had to be an A+ student all the time. I went to school to socialize. The friends that I had were close friends. I think quality over quantity is more important when it comes to knowing people. I got along with almost everyone though, and I feel like teachers loved me.

I've always been super organized. I would set my clothes out for school the night before and have my binder organized by subject. I was never late for class either. If you're not five minutes early, you're late.

My favorite part of school was being involved in cheerleading. It gave me something to look forward to throughout the school day and week. Being involved with cheerleading from seventh grade through twelfth grade gave me consistency that I like. Change is one thing I don't deal with well.

Starting a new school year always gave me anxiety because I didn't know what to expect. Even as an adult, I can tell that change still affects my well-being and sense of peace.

Growing up I had separation anxiety until around third grade. I don't know what caused it or how it went away. I went to a few therapy sessions growing up and was on medication for a little bit, but I'm not sure if either of those helped.

- **female, 6W7**

121

ENNEAGRAM TYPE SEVEN
The High-Energy & Adventurous Student

*"In every life we have some trouble
but when you worry you make it double.
Don't worry, be happy.
Don't worry, be happy now."*

- *Don't Worry Be Happy*, Bobby McFerrin

charming

curious

fun-loving

impulsive

distracted

confident

passionate

optimistic

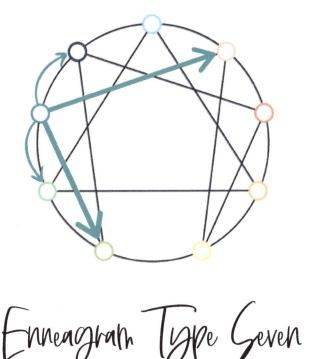

Enneagram Type Seven

Sevens desire freedom and exploration. They crave adventure and new opportunities, and they want to experience all that life has to offer. Sevens are extroverted, upbeat, optimistic, and spontaneous. They are always up for a last-minute adventure.

Sevens keep full calendars. They prefer vacations with a full hour by hour and minute by minute itinerary so they are sure to make time for everything. Sevens want to have a wide variety of choices and fun experiences; because of this, they keep their options open, are slow to commit to plans (in case something better pops up) and do their absolute best to avoid missing out on anything fun.

Sevens seek all of this adventure as a way to avoid pain, negative thoughts and feelings, or serious conversations. They don't want to feel trapped or limited. They don't want to be bored or sad. Sevens will crack a joke at an inappropriate time to lighten the mood. They may laugh when someone gets hurt, and then check to make sure they are okay. They may create a humorous scene in the middle of getting in trouble with hopes of receiving a lesser punishment.

Sevens minds are constantly wandering and thinking about what's next. They anticipate the future and get extremely excited when they realize all of the possibilities that await them. They throw themselves into action and put their plans in motion. This can cause them to miss out on the present moment. They are looking forward to the next adventure so much so that they often find that they miss out on their current one.

Other types, even other Sevens, can find it challenging to be around average or unhealthy Sevens. Their scattered energy and endless busyness can grow very tiresome. This frustrates the Seven and they eventually move on to something or someone new. Sevens have long lists of friends, but the relationships are generally surface level. Sevens may find that they don't have many deep or genuine friendships, they have a phone full of contacts who are looking to have fun.

IN A NUTSHELL...

The Seven student is an adventurer. They are social butterflies and class clowns. They are full of energy and always want to have a good time. School may not be their favorite place, but they will try to make it fun, so they don't experience boredom.

Core Fear - Being limited or bored, being overwhelmed, feeling pain or sadness
Core Desire - To always be happy and fully content
Focus - Finding the bright side or silver lining in situations and circumstances. Reframing anything negative.
Goal - To feel completely satisfied each day.

Biggest Struggle - Gluttony

Sevens typically feel a huge emptiness inside of them and they want to fill that hole with experiences and adventures. They believe that constantly seeking new opportunities will give them a feeling of contentment and satisfaction.

CHARACTERISTICS

Sevens are playful and spontaneous. They are the life of any party. The fun doesn't begin until the Seven arrives. They are extroverted and positive; they are upbeat and fun.

Sevens can be impatient when they feel that others are slowing them down or are unable to keep up. They don't want to feel stuck or trapped somewhere so they always have a plan B or an escape plan.

Sevens don't want to be tied down or commit to anything long term. Commitments or long-term plans prevent them from having an open schedule to attend any last-minute adventure that comes up.

Sevens are experience-oriented, not so much achievement-oriented. Sevens enjoy activities for what they are, not necessarily the achievement or recognition that come along with it. A Seven will run a marathon to say they did it, not for the medal or a possible reward or personal record at the end.

Sevens are storytellers. They are also excellent at reframing anything negative. They can turn a bad situation into a positive one pretty easily. They are quick learners and they love to debate, even if they are completely aware that they know less than their opponent.

They have a lot of new and exciting ideas, but they rarely follow through with them. Oftentimes they get bored, think of a new idea, and move on.

COMMUNICATION STYLE

Sevens are talkative. They are social butterflies. There probably isn't a seat in the classroom that will hinder their ability to chat with a peer. They are energetic and can be hyperactive.

They like to keep the conversation moving. They don't like lulls or awkward silence. They also don't like to discuss anything serious, so they will interrupt, change the subject, or dodge the conversation as needed.

Sevens may easily find themselves going off on a tangent. Their minds are restless and this shows up in their conversation. They struggle with serious topics or anything negative, so if they don't have an opportunity to change the subject, they will do their best to avoid those conversations completely. If a conversation gets too deep or painful, don't be surprised if they interrupt with a funny story or joke in an attempt to change the subject, lighten the mood, or shift the focus.

Sevens are very enthusiastic and generally excited about life. They demonstrate their enthusiasm in conversations by speaking with their hands.

Below are a few suggestions on how to effectively communicate with a High-Energy and Adventurous Student:

- They may not be able to say 'yes' right away. Commitment can be difficult.
- It's hard for Sevens to explain what they are thinking because their minds move so fast.
- They can feel rejected if they share an exciting thought or idea and it gets shut down.
- They are prone to interrupting, but it's not to be rude, it's because they are excited about something you said. It's a sign that they are listening.
- They can be sensitive, even if they don't show that side of them.
- Sevens have to feel like something was their idea, otherwise they can rebel, run away from, or avoid the task or commitment.

LEARNING STYLE

Sevens are the complete opposite of Sixes. Routines and structure bore them to tears. They like for things to be new and exciting. They don't mind a change in plans or an unexpected substitute. In fact, when there is a sub, a Seven may even come up with the idea to switch names with another student, just for fun.

Type Seven students are motivated by stimulation, adventure, action, fun, opportunity, and freedom. They are curious and full of energy, but they can become bored pretty quickly. Because of this, they want to be moving and on the go. If you can set up frequent movement breaks (that are predictable and routine for your Sixes) you'll help Sevens stay engaged during class.

Sevens enjoy learning if it's a topic of interest, but they may struggle to complete assignments. They may also struggle with engaging in or contributing to classroom discussions, but they do love to experiment and try new things.

They enjoy the social aspect of group projects, but finishing a long-term assignment can be challenging because Sevens get bored and want to move on. They are great at short-term projects. Sevens are excellent team players, but they most likely won't step up or volunteer to be the leader of the group. However, Sevens don't like to be told what to do. If a Seven is in a group with a bossy leader, or a class with a controlling teacher, they may struggle.

Sevens don't need to see the full picture or watch others before jumping in themselves. They get right to it. They don't enjoy tedious busy work or assignments that are extremely detailed. They are quick learners and self-starters.

One tip for the Sevens would be to set realistic goals and celebrate each success. After the celebration, then they can get started on the next thing. This will help them with productivity and achievement, instead of quitting something before they finish.

WORK ETHIC

Sevens are excellent multitaskers. You may notice them doodling or drawing while taking notes. Just so you know, they are paying attention; this strategy helps them focus on the material and topic of discussion. With that being said, Sevens are also very easily distracted. Finding ways to keep them engaged and focused will promote learning and a deeper understanding of the material.

Sevens enjoy the unpredictable. They welcome change and enjoy when their teachers shake things up. Anytime a lesson can involve movement, rotations, experiments, or any other engaging tasks, Sevens are all in.

Sevens are quick learners, and they easily see and understand connections between different ideas or topics. They work well with others and enjoy group assignments. Seven students desire freedom. If they have an opportunity to learn without being confined or limited by a lot of unnecessary rules, they are more likely to excel.

Report card feedback may say: Student works well with any of the other students in the class, student talks excessively and is easily distracted, or student displays a positive attitude in the classroom.

PREFERRED CLASSROOM ENVIRONMENT

Seven students desire a fast-paced working environment. They want an energetic and enthusiastic atmosphere. Sevens avoid negative thoughts and feelings, and they may feel trapped in the classroom if the energy isn't positive. They want the classroom to be fun and engaging. Remember, Sevens fear being bored, so school can be a very difficult place if they have to sit still, take notes, and listen to lectures all day long. Seven students need excitement. They need interaction.

Remind Sevens that life isn't always fun and games, and that sometimes they do have to be serious. However, also remind them that life is always what they make it. If they are feeling bored, they have the power within them to appropriately change the narrative. Then, elaborate to explain that disrupting the class would not be an appropriate way for them to change the narrative.

WINGS

The wings attached to Type Seven are The Questioning and Loyal Student (Type Six) and The Opinionated and Confident Student (Type Eight). These wings can be abbreviated as 7W6 and 7W8.

THE 7W6

The Type Seven with the Six wing is more outgoing, creative, and playful. They care what others think about them. They want to enjoy all that life has to offer and they want to experience it with others. When struggling, the 7W6 becomes less focused and their energy and attention becomes more scattered. They desire more relationships and material things to distract them from their negative thoughts and emotions and feelings of boredom. This wing is inspiring because they are joyful, passionate, engaging, and fun. They are loyal and committed to their friends and family.

THE 7W8

The Type Seven with the Eight wing is more assertive and confident. They are ambitious and have a quick mind and an intense energy. Unlike the 7W6, they aren't worried about what others think of them. When struggling, the 7W8 becomes more direct and demanding, and can turn into a workaholic. They become adrenaline seekers and they can be aggressive towards anyone who stands in their way or challenges their plans or ideas. This wing is inspiring because they don't recognize a failure. When something doesn't work the way they want it to or expect it to, they are able to reframe it and see it from a new perspective. This creates space for them to try again.

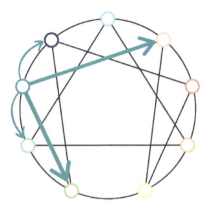

THINGS TO LEARN

One of the biggest things that Sevens can learn is patience, and that real happiness can be found in anything and anywhere. Happiness and joy are readily available. Sevens will also benefit when they learn to think before they act. Sevens are so quick to move and act. Sometimes, slowing down and thinking first will help them to process and make better decisions. They can also learn that one way to gain wisdom is by facing your fears and experiencing negative things. Experience is one of our greatest teachers.

IN STRESS

In stress, a Seven moves to an average to an unhealthy Type One. They can place limitations and restrictions on themselves in order to become more productive. They can become perfectionistic and more critical of themselves and others. They become irritable and frustrated when others prevent them from having fun. Sevens in stress will notice and point out imperfections in themselves and their work or others. They will start to place higher expectations on themselves and others, and they may begin to micromanage others who they believe aren't being responsible.

IN GROWTH

In growth, a Seven moves to a healthy Type Five. They become more grounded and focused. They are able to accept life for what it is and accept the times of joy as well as the times of sorrow. In growth, Sevens are able to relax. They allow their minds time to rest which gives them clarity and creativity. They can sit with uncomfortable feelings and stop using their minds to distract themselves from life.

LEVELS OF DEVELOPMENT

Healthy levels:

Level 1 - (at their best) They are extremely grateful for what they have. They love life and are in awe of its wonder and beauty. They appreciate the simple and little things. They are joyous.
Level 2 - They are extroverted. They are excited and enthusiastic about life and its experiences. Everything is rejuvenating. They are eager, spontaneous, full of life, and happy.
Level 3 - They have many talents and achieve things easily. They do many things well. They are productive and practical. They have a variety of interests.

Average levels:

Level 4 - When they become restless, they want more options and choices. They are adventurous and wise, but less focused. They always look for something new and aren't satisfied with their regular routines. They constantly try to keep up with the latest trends.
Level 5 - They are always on the go and constantly in motion. They are unable to determine what they actually need and are unable to say no. They fear being bored. They commit to many things and come up with many ideas. They have little follow through.
Level 6 - They are self-centered and greedy. They are very materialistic and feel as though they never have enough. They are bossy and demanding. They aren't satisfied with their current situation.

Unhealthy levels:

Level 7 - They can be impulsive. They are offensive and can be abusive. They do not know when to stop or when enough is enough.
Level 8 - They have intense mood swings and act on their impulses. They don't deal with their anxieties. They get easily frustrated. They can become out of control.
Level 9 - They live in panic and can become claustrophobic. They give up on themselves and their dreams. They are exhausted and can suffer from depression. They can turn to self-destructive behaviors. They could suffer from bipolar disorder.

DEFENSE MECHANISM

The defense mechanism for the Seven is rationalization. Sevens use rationalization to avoid owning their real intentions, motivations, and behaviors in order to maintain a self-image of being alright or okay. Rationalization is a way to reframe any situation, so their behavior and attitude is justified. They want to create space between themselves and painful emotions or situations, and they will not take responsibility for their unacceptable thoughts, feelings, and behaviors. They re-frame everything to be positive. Their ability to re-frame and create new stories with endless possibilities allows them to tune out whatever is going on in the present moment with all of the restrictions and limitations and live in a limitless world.

CHILDHOOD PATTERNS

The Seven child feels disconnected from the parent who is supposed to be loving and nurturing. For some this is mom, for others this is dad, and others, it's a parent-like figure or guardian. This leaves them feeling neglected and emotionally cut off. As a result, the Seven child feels the need to nurture and care for themselves. Self-reliance manifests and leaves the Seven child feeling that they can only rely on themselves to get the things that they need to be happy and satisfied. The message they hear, whether directly or indirectly, from caregivers or authority figures is: "you are on your own to take care of your needs."

The Seven child distracts themselves with things that bring them pleasure whenever they start to feel a negative emotion or experience an ounce of boredom. They feel solely responsible for creating a world of pleasant thoughts and experiences in order to replace painful thoughts or feelings. Their minds are wonderful and can make anything better because they have endless experiences waiting for them in their imagination. The Seven child often feels unsatisfied which keeps them in a perpetual state of seeking new and exciting adventures to fill their feelings of emptiness. Seven children are like Peter Pan. They truly believe in magic, and they create their own Neverland.

TRIGGERS FOR CONFLICT

When Sevens are triggered, they are going to avoid any negative or unpleasant situations by thinking, reframing, and imagining happier experiences. Sevens will rationalize and justify their behavior. They will reframe the events in order to make themselves look and sound better, and they will likely blame others for running the fun.

Conflict in Sevens may be triggered if they feel that they are being dismissed or aren't being taken seriously. Sevens don't like to complete mundane tasks, so asking them to do something may be a trigger. They don't like to be criticized or forced to deal with painful or serious situations or circumstances. They can't stand to be around people who are always negative and overly critical.

A HOW-TO GUIDE FOR THE HIGH-ENERGY AND ADVENTUROUS STUDENT

- Help them to understand that it's important to live in the moment and be fully present. The next adventure will come, and they don't want to miss out on their current experience.
- Let them know that experiencing tough emotions will make them stronger.
- Remind them that they aren't on their own and that they will be taken care of.
- It's important to pay attention to their level of development:
  - A healthy Type Seven is joyful, spontaneous, and grateful for the things that they have.
  - An average Type Seven is restless and always has to be on the go. They are unsure of what they actually need.
  - An unhealthy Type Seven can be impulsive and offensive. They have intense mood swings and can become easily frustrated.
- If a student is at a healthy level, encourage and reassure them that they are on the right path.
- If a student is at an unhealthy level, pay attention to their environment. What may be triggering their negative behaviors and attitudes? Find ways to work with their strengths and make them more confident.
- Pushing, nagging, or focusing on their mistakes and flaws will more than likely only make matters worse. If needed, seek professional help and guidance.

FAMOUS ENNEAGRAM SEVENS

- Robin Williams
- Britney Spears
- Conan O'Brien
- Ted Danson
- Sacha Baron Cohen
- Dick Van Dyke
- John F. Kennedy
- Tigger (*Winnie the Pooh*)

TYPE SEVEN QUESTIONNAIRE

Does the student:

☐ enjoy trying new things?

☐ desire attention and enjoy the spotlight?

☐ have a hard time sitting still?

☐ seem to be happy and upbeat all of the time?

☐ enjoy telling funny stories and jokes?

☐ struggle to finish a project or task before moving on to something new?

☐ seem really curious and enjoy learning new things?

☐ avoid difficult or serious conversations or situations?

☐ struggle to process their emotions?

☐ seem to be friends with everyone and make new friends easily?

ADULT REFLECTIONS ON BEING A HIGH-ENERGY AND ADVENTUROUS STUDENT

1. I really didn't like the structure of school, and it was boring to see the same people day after day. I needed more freedom. I felt like I was suffocating.
2. My senior year of high school I took as many periods off as I could in order to leave early. I was a good student, but I couldn't wait to graduate.
3. I was very involved and hyper pretty much all of the time.
4. I was popular and got voted class clown year after year.
5. I was rebellious and was frequently in trouble.
6. School was fun and I had a lot of learning experiences, but I was overly concerned with alcohol, sex, and drugs my junior and senior year.
7. I never got my work done because in most of my classes I just talked with my friends. My teachers always had to separate me from them.
8. I had a lot of friends from a bunch of different cliques. I loved school. I really was friends with everyone.
9. I liked to stay busy so I always had an after-school job, and I hung out with my boyfriend when I wasn't working.
10. I was very loud, hyper, and excitable. I acted crazy and psycho because I was the goofball of my friend group. I always wanted to make them laugh so I was overly dramatic and theatrical.

WHAT BEING A HIGH-ENERGY AND ADVENTUROUS STUDENT WAS LIKE:

In elementary school I was a very, very quiet and sweet kid. I did what I was told and even became a teacher's pet. I made all As in elementary school. I had a couple of good friends, but I wasn't 'popular' by any means. I just stayed in my lane.

In middle school I started to get more Bs in subjects like reading, English, social sciences, and science. But I loved math, like LOVED it! I thought I was going to be an engineer because I loved it so much. It just was easy for me to understand. I got it and knew it better than anything else. English has always been tough for me, and still is. I made decent grades. I definitely was an average student making mostly As and Bs. I didn't pay attention to any class, really, only math. I loved math. Algebra was for sure my favorite subject because I loved to solve problems and there was a clear path on how to get the answer through a formula.

I was very easily distracted. I still am! In middle school I taunted my teachers and was very social in class. I was in the 'popular' group and wanted to seem 'cool' in front of my classmates which meant that I had to be mean to the teachers. I was always getting in trouble in classes with my friends because we talked so much. I got kicked out of class a lot, got pink slips, and had to run extra laps because my friends and I just wouldn't stop talking. The first C I made was in high school Spanish. I didn't put a lot of effort in. In high school I wasn't as big of a troublemaker, but I didn't pay attention in any classes. Cheating is what got me through school. It was very hard for me to want to learn.

By the time I got to high school I didn't care about any subject really. And I never wanted to put in the effort to learn. When I took an engineering class, I realized it was too hard and I didn't care for it so I cheated my way through it. However, when I got to college, I loved learning because I took classes I wanted to take. My major was communication studies.

Socially, I was very insecure about being too loud or annoying in middle school and I got bullied a lot because of it. So, I felt like I had to make myself smaller to fit in. If I said anything that was 'weird' or 'annoying,' my friends would say something, and I wouldn't speak for the rest of the day or night when we were together after school.

They made me feel very small and I felt like what I had to say wasn't important. So, in high school I drifted from those people, I got a boyfriend, and I found a guy friend group that I'm still best friends with. I felt like I could be myself around the guys.

When I got to college, I found genuine people who liked me for me, so my confidence grew exponentially because I wasn't afraid to be myself. A lot of people can't handle loud people, but I found people who loved me for who I am.

- **Samantha Carpenter, 7W6**

School was easy for me. I didn't have to work that hard to retain the information. Now that I'm an adult and I understand the Enneagram, I wonder if that's related to being in the Thinking Center. One of my daughters is a Nine, and school does not come as easily for her. I watch her work really hard to do well. I love and admire her work ethic.

My dad was an educator and that affected my perspective of education. Going to school excited me. I really loved learning; I wanted to learn. I grew up in a large family and my parents couldn't say yes to every request; this made me want to get a good education so that I could get the things I wanted in life.

I started high school at 5'9 and was probably considered more of a nerd than anything. I did pretty well in school even though I was a huge procrastinator. The stress of a deadline allowed me to get organized and get the job done. I didn't skip class and I always did my work, but that's probably because I had great relationships with my teachers; they all knew my dad. But I was voted class clown a few different times.

In my sophomore year, I learned about a student exchange program, and I applied to go to Brazil. There were 5 kids in my family; it was crowded. I was 16 and I wanted an adventure. So, I went, and Brazil was incredible. I was so enthralled with that lifestyle and the culture that when I got back, I wanted to return, but my parents put a kibosh on that and made me go to college. My first two years of college I kinda just enjoyed life and deprioritized my education. I played sports and joined a fraternity. I didn't know what I wanted to do, and I didn't take that time too seriously.

- **male, 7W8**

ENNEAGRAM TYPE EIGHT
The Opinionated & Confident Student

*"No, I'll stand my ground,
won't be turned around.
And I'll keep this world from draggin' me down,
gonna stand my ground."*

- I Won't Back Down, Tom Petty

protective

decisive

honest

skeptical

confrontational

strong

bold

empowering

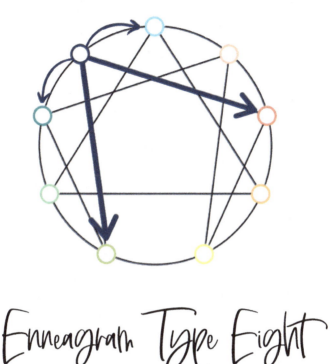

Enneagram Type Eight

Before we really dig into the Eight, I want to preface that Eights can have a bad reputation and it really doesn't have to be that way. Average to unhealthy Eights can be quite challenging, intimidating, mean, rude, and unpleasant, but every type has a negative side. Eights are just more open and upfront about theirs. They don't hide it. Healthy Eights are amazing. Everyone wants a healthy Eight in their corner (actually, everyone wants a healthy version of every type in their corner). But for the purpose of this section, my hope is that if you do have an average or unhealthy Eight in your life, that you can gain some understanding about where they are coming from. That way, you can be the one to change. You can stop taking things personally and ultimately, do the work to improve that relationship. When Eights are responded to in their language, the challenges subside.

And now let's take this a step further and mention female Eights, because female Eights can be seen as some of the most difficult people to get along with. But truthfully, everything is about perspective. Men are allowed to be bold and tough. Women, not so much. Assertive and intimidating males are called leaders. Assertive and intimidating females are called, well, you know.

Eights are the challengers of the Enneagram, but they are also the protectors. They are the first in line to protest, whether that's marching and taking it to the streets, or going right to the top of an organization with a phone call or letter explaining their position and offering suggestions about how to make everything right. They are also the first to run anyone over who gets in their way. Do you see how their level of health plays an important role?

They seek justice and equality for all. They protect the innocent and the weak. They defend the defenseless and they typically have a soft spot for babies, smaller children, and animals.

Eights will stand up to their teachers and defend their classmates against bullies, but Eights may also be the bully.

Eights are assertive and rational problem solvers. At their best, they are advocates for those in need, inspiring, and encouraging. But, they sometimes get into trouble because they can come across as rude or insensitive. Eights want to be independent, and they want to be seen as someone who is very capable and influential.

Eights keep their commitments and value authenticity and integrity. They have no problem speaking their mind which can be intimidating to others. They believe that backing down from any sort of conflict is a sign of weakness. They also believe that vulnerability is a sign of weakness.

Beneath this bold and tough exterior, an Eight is a genuine and compassionate person. They stand up for and defend others, and they have a strong sense of justice. People should be treated equally and fairly, and they aren't afraid to step up and call someone out who is being unjust. They are natural leaders and will protect others without concern for how it will affect them personally.

Eights desire control and avoid feeling weak or vulnerable by aggressively confronting a situation they feel needs to change. Others might interpret this as insensitivity or rudeness, but the Eights' intense fear of feeling weak or vulnerable causes them to suppress their emotions and try to control the situation anyway.

They may even end up sacrificing the chance to have close relationships with others because that requires vulnerability. Because of this, Eights end up feeling incomplete and may find that they are not able to enjoy a meaningful connection with someone. At their best, they will set aside their fears and allow people to truly get to know who they are. When they show others who they really are underneath their rough and tumble exterior, they are better equipped to be a leader and empower others. In order to be accepted into an Eights world, respect must be earned.

Try not to be intimidated by an Eight though. In their minds, conflict equals connection.

IN A NUTSHELL...

The Eight student is a challenger. They can be intense and insensitive. They can be fiercely protective of their friends and family, and they will also go to bat for someone who is unable to protect themselves. Eights recognize a weakness a mile away and they want nothing to do with being weak themselves.

Eights are confrontational. They enjoy it. Sometimes, they will pick a fight just to see what you are made of and if you will stand up for yourself. If you do, you have earned their respect. Eights don't back down and they don't want you to back down, either.

Core Fear - Being manipulated or controlled by others; being weak, powerless, or vulnerable
Core Desire - To protect themselves and others, and have control over their own life
Focus - Gaining power, control, and independence.
Goal - Demonstrate that they are independent and in control.

Biggest Struggle - Lust

Eights lust after control and power. They can be intense and tend to push themselves onto others, or run others over, in order to get what they want.

CHARACTERISTICS

Eights are assertive and independent. They want freedom and control over their choices and their life. They want to be self-reliant. Eights are natural leaders. They can easily take control of a room because they speak and act with authority. If you tell an Eight they can't do something, sit back and watch them prove you wrong.

Eights have incredible vision, and they step up and take action; when they move forward with something, they are all in. Eights don't do something halfway. If they give their word and agree to do something, they are going to do it. Honor is very important to an Eight.

Eights are intense and direct, and they expect others to engage with them the same way. It's common for an Eight to keep raising their energy and pushing your buttons until they feel that your reaction has met their standards. Remember the Eights' math equation, conflict equals connection.

Eights are confident and can be egocentric. They can't stand when others aren't being genuine, and they can sense dishonesty or phoniness pretty quickly.

Eights are decisive. They are able to make a decision and stick to it. If they make the wrong decision, they can handle the fallout and backlash.

COMMUNICATION STYLE

Eight students mean business. They say what they mean. They aren't worried about hurt feelings and they certainly don't sugarcoat anything. They are direct. They are truthful, even if the truth isn't pleasant.

Eights are commanding. They get energy from conflict and confrontation. If they become bored, they may very well make a controversial comment just to watch what happens next.

A pro tip: Eights will respect you if you hold your ground with them. If you cave, or change your stance to get out of the conflict or conversation, you will appear weak. Appearing weak to an Eight will not necessarily improve your relationship.

Educators and parents, you need to be firm and consistent with your Eight students. Do your best to avoid power struggles with them and try not to react to their anger. Do your best to keep your composure and stand your ground.

Below are a few suggestions on how to effectively communicate with a Opinionated and Confident Student:

- They rarely depend on others for anything. If they ask you for help, they appreciate and trust you.
- They do feel empathy, but they aren't likely to show it. They are direct and honest. You'll never have to guess what they mean or how they feel.
- Expectations are difficult. They don't like to be told what to do or how to do something. They want freedom and independence.
- If they get passionate or excited about something, they can get

loud and may even start to sound angry. But they aren't angry, they are just excited.

- Eights are sensitive. They rarely show it, but they have feelings, just like the rest of us.

LEARNING STYLE

Eight students love a good debate. If you can find a way to schedule a debate in your subject, you will speak to the Eights in the room. They can argue just for the sake of arguing.

They are independent learners. They typically don't require much supervision once they are in their groove. Eights don't necessarily enjoy group work because that can take away their freedom to do things how they want. However, they are natural leaders. They would be able to lead the group and make sure that the work is split up evenly and completed well. Remember, once they commit to something, they are all in. Their willingness to lead oftentimes helps them to have an integral part in the learning process.

Eights like to make sure that their presence is known. During class discussions, they will most likely give their opinion, even if it may be inappropriate or unpopular. This is also true for classroom rules and procedures. If a rule doesn't seem fair, they will most likely challenge it. If the rules aren't enforced consistently, they may stand up for someone who gets in trouble, especially if another student did the same thing without consequence.

In addition, if a rule is not enforced then it simply doesn't exist. The Eight student will push boundaries and test their limits. This is mainly to see how much they are able to get away with. If you have fair rules, and you consistently enforce them, then this should not be a problem.

WORK ETHIC

Eight students need to be challenged. If they are bored, they are likely to find something else to do instead. However, if something doesn't line up with their thoughts or beliefs, the Eight student will be the first to challenge it and make it known that they disagree.

Eight students are intelligent, but they can be stubborn and bullheaded. They may not demonstrate their full understanding if they don't see the point. They may refuse to do homework if they already understand the topic and gladly accept the deduction in their grade. They may skip class if they have something more important to do or feel that the lesson or subject isn't necessary for what they want to do in life.

On the other hand, though, Eight students may also want to excel. If they care about their grades and schoolwork, then they will do well because those things are important to them. If something is important to an Eight, they get it done. If it's not, they will find something to do that is important.

Report card feedback may say: Student is always looking for new ways to be challenged, student could demonstrate more respect for authority, or student enjoys taking on leadership roles in the classroom.

PREFERRED CLASSROOM ENVIRONMENT

Eight students stand up and protect the underdog. They fight for justice, fairness, and equality. That being said, they prefer an environment that has fair and consistent rules. They don't want to be around teachers who show favoritism or bend the rules for some students, but not for others. It doesn't matter if a student never, ever gets in trouble. If they break a rule, the consequence should be the same as the student who is in the principal's office regularly.

Eights love to challenge others. Any time they have an opportunity to debate, they're on it. They have a lot of confidence, and they love to prove others wrong. Set them up for success and give them a debatable topic every now and then, regardless of the subject. Every subject can get creative in order to have a good debate.

They want to be in a highly engaging environment. They like whole class discussions and frequent movement. Eight students want to be involved. They don't want to sit in the classroom and listen to the teacher the entire class period. To them, it's easy enough to read the textbook or research the topic at home and get the information they need that way. Challenge them in class. Involve them in class. Give them experiences that they can't get on their own somewhere else.

WINGS

The wings attached to Type Eight are The High-Energy and Adventurous Student (Type Seven) and The Calm and Peaceful Student (Type Nine). These wings can be abbreviated as 8W7 and 8W9.

THE 8W7

The Type Eight with the Seven wing tends to be more blunt, intense, and demanding. They ooze with confidence and have a lot of energy. They want others to be like them: direct, quick, and assertive. When struggling, their attention turns to gaining power and control. This is what they focus on. They can become more impatient, impulsive, and demanding. They turn into adrenaline seekers, and they can be aggressive towards anyone who stands in their way or challenges them. This wing is inspiring because they are a force. They can see what can and needs to be done, and they are able to create a path forward for others.

THE 8W9

The Type Eight with the Nine wing is more steady, patient, and compassionate. They aren't as aggressive and they prefer more comfort and peace. When struggling, they can become more intimidating and temperamental. They become more aggressive at school, work, or extracurricular activities, and more passive at home. This wing is inspiring because they are able to motivate and inspire others to excel with their natural leadership abilities.

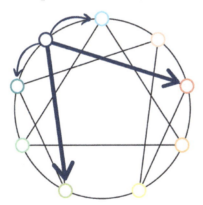

THINGS TO LEARN

Eight students would benefit from learning that their directness and assertiveness can be intimidating to those who are not Eights. That doesn't mean that others are necessarily weak, it just means that they aren't as intense. It would also help for Eights to learn to control their temper. It's okay to be angry, but figuring out where the anger is stemming from will be huge for them. This will also help them learn that it is okay to be vulnerable.

IN STRESS

In stress, an Eight moves to an average to an unhealthy Type Five. They tend to observe more than participate. They can withdraw and isolate themselves from others and become more secretive. They may begin to detach from their emotions and develop a 'know-it-all' attitude, so they are always prepared and on the offense. They tend to use their knowledge and intellect to belittle others, and they can become harsher and more cynical.

IN GROWTH

In growth, an Eight moves to a healthy Type Two. They are able to create a path forward for others. They become more thoughtful and caring of others and others' thoughts, feelings, and opinions. They open up and show their vulnerable side more easily. They create space to have more empathy and compassion for others. They are more considerate and will begin to put the needs of others before their own. They step up to the plate to help or serve.

LEVELS OF DEVELOPMENT

Healthy levels:

Level 1 - (at their best) They could become a true hero and gain historical greatness. They are willing to put themselves in danger or harm's way for their vision and the greater good. They are courageous and merciful.
Level 2 - They are self-assertive and strong. They are self-confident. They stand up for what they believe in and what they want. They are passionate and have a 'can do' attitude.
Level 3 - They are natural leaders. They are decisive and authoritative. They make things happen. They are protectors and providers. They are honorable and they take initiative. Others look up to them.

Average levels:

Level 4 - They are self-sufficient and independent. They are resourceful and pragmatic. They take risks and are very hardworking. They can deny their own emotional needs to get the job done.
Level 5 - They become controlling and can dominate their environment. They want to be the leader and have others following and supporting them. They are boastful. They are bossy and what they say goes. They are proud and egocentric. Their vision is pushed on to others, and they don't see or treat others as equals.

Level 6 - They can be extremely combative. They will intimidate others to get their way. They are confrontational and turn friends into enemies. They do not back down. They use threats to get followers and they keep others insecure. This treatment may cause their followers to rise up against them.

Unhealthy levels:

Level 7 - These Eights can become criminals and con-artists. They are cold, immoral, and can be violent. They are ruthless when they think someone is trying to control them. They can become dictators.
Level 8 - They believe they are invincible. They live in a fantasy about their power and ability to prevail. They are reckless and overextend themselves.
Level 9 - If they find themselves in a threatening or dangerous situation, they may destroy everything in their path and everyone who has not conformed to their beliefs or visions. They are vengeful and may have sociopathic tendencies. They are antisocial and can bring serious harm to others.

DEFENSE MECHANISM

The defense mechanism for the Eight is denial. Eights use denial to avoid being weak and vulnerable and to maintain a self-image of being strong and confident. They believe that they are invincible. Eights use denial to forget or completely ignore unpleasant things. They are easily able to refocus their energy and attention. Vulnerable feelings are swept to the side and not paid attention to. Eights will deny that they were hurtful or insensitive to others because they won't allow themselves to remember that anything unpleasant occurred. They are the protectors, so if they have caused harm to someone, they aren't going to easily accept their wrongdoing. They deny that they are human just like the rest of us: able to be betrayed, harmed, controlled, and vulnerable.

CHILDHOOD PATTERNS

The Eight child believes that the world is an aggressive and antagonistic place. They think that only those who are tough, smart, and strong will survive. They witness the weak, innocent, and vulnerable being taken advantage of and they do not want to become like those people. They learn to develop thick skin, a tough exterior, and a shield to protect their hearts. They feel that this protective armor is necessary for survival.

Eight children can be very confrontational, challenging, and rebellious.

They do not want to be controlled or challenged, so they will control others first. They can dominate a room with their intense energy. Eight children do not trust others easily and they worry a great deal about being betrayed.

Many Eights are betrayed in some way as children. They lose their innocence at a young age and decide that they need their protective armor from that moment on.

TRIGGERS FOR CONFLICT

When Eights are triggered, they will pull apart information quickly and make a decision about how to move forward. They may feel anger inside of them that they must release as soon as possible. In order to protect themselves from showing vulnerability and being controlled or harmed, they are going to turn to their trusted strategies to get them through the situation. They may seek advice from someone they trust, and they will most likely let go of those who they do not respect. Eights discard people easily.

Conflict in Eights may be triggered when people aren't direct with them and try to go behind their back. If an Eight sees someone being taken advantage of or an injustice isn't being responded to, they may feel triggered and step up themselves to solve the problem. Eights can feel triggered when others don't own up to their behaviors and actions, when others aren't direct, truthful, and straightforward, or when they have been blindsided, manipulated, or betrayed.

A HOW-TO GUIDE FOR THE OPINIONATED AND CONFIDENT STUDENT

- Understand that when Eight students show their anger, more likely than not, they are sad and upset about something else They don't know how to process or discuss their emotions, because to them, being vulnerable is a sign of weakness.
- Remember that Eights respect those who stand their ground and don't back down.
- Try to give Eight students ways to positively lead. They may try to find negative ways to demonstrate their power and control.
- It's important to pay attention to their level of development:
    - A healthy Type Eight is confident, passionate, and a natural leader. They do things for the greater good.
    - An average Type Eight can be controlling and boastful. They can dominate their environment.
    - An unhealthy Type Eight can be vengeful or violent if they feel that they are being controlled.
- If a student is at a healthy level, encourage and reassure them that they are on the right path.
- If a student is at an unhealthy level, pay attention to their environment. What may be triggering their negative behaviors and attitudes? Find ways to work with their strengths and make them more confident.
- Pushing, nagging, or focusing on their mistakes and flaws will more than likely only make matters worse. If needed, seek professional help and guidance.

FAMOUS ENNEAGRAM EIGHTS

- Martin Luther King, Jr.
- Barbara Walters
- Serena Williams
- Winston Churchill
- Franklin D. Roosevelt
- Chelsea Handler
- Aretha Franklin
- Katniss Everdeen (*Hunger Games*)

TYPE EIGHT QUESTIONNAIRE

Does the student:

☐ seem really confident?

☐ seem to enjoy confrontation?

☐ give teachers and caregivers a hard time?

☐ stand up for themselves and others?

☐ tell other children what to do?

☐ refuse to back down from conflict?

☐ demonstrate leadership qualities?

☐ show anger easily and freely?

☐ make you, and others, aware of their presence?

☐ figure out ways to get what they want?

ADULT REFLECTIONS ON BEING AN OPINIONATED AND CONFIDENT STUDENT

1. I decided that I was done with school long before middle school.
2. I had a problem with authority since early elementary school and was earning money at age 8. I dropped out as soon as I could and began working full time.
3. I was definitely standoffish, and it irritated me when I had to do work that I thought was pointless.
4. At times I was condescending to my teachers, but I did have a few teachers who were capable of challenging me. I loved them.
5. I smoked, skipped school, and got suspended. I ran away every weekend, and then finally ran away for good when I was 15.
6. I was friends with everyone. I was a social butterfly, and I had a lot of confidence.
7. I really enjoyed pushing my teachers' buttons. I can't tell you how many times I got kicked out of class.
8. I was always a quick learner, but I was so bored. I aced all of my tests and would devour textbooks on my own. Because of that, I found classes under stimulating and often skipped them.
9. I joined almost every club or group that I could because I wanted to be away from home as much as possible.
10. I was extremely driven, and I had a lot of fun. I made good grades and played all of the sports. I had to be the best at everything.
11. When I started high school, I told my teachers that I was not going to do homework or study. I told them that they had me for 8 hours and that was it. And I didn't do any homework, nor did I study, and I still got great grades.

WHAT BEING AN OPINIONATED AND CONFIDENT STUDENT WAS LIKE:

Everyone that I have ever met said that I am conflict-avoidant and stubborn. I am the perfect combination of Eight and Nine.

I never did my homework if I already knew the concept. I took the grade penalty because I wasn't going to do more to prove that I already knew something. I dominated the conversation a lot in school with my teachers, although I didn't necessarily mean to do that. Looking back, I feel sorry for the teachers I did that to. But at the same time, I know that I taught them a few things.

I had a lot of self-esteem issues in high school. I craved leadership. I needed leadership. In high school, I decided that I wanted to become a high school math teacher. I didn't have any leadership qualities of my own, but I wanted to be for kids what I needed myself. I did, however, start a bible study in high school with my core group of friends. That put me in a position to be a leader and a teacher. I really enjoyed starting that.

Like I said, I had a low self-esteem, and I didn't really know who I was. My emotional maturity was low, and I felt like I needed to prove to everyone that I could do whatever it was that I needed to do. My voice needed to be heard and I needed to prove that I could be a leader. I was very stubborn (I still am). I was very immature and was at unhealthy levels of development.

I was nice to everyone, but I didn't really pay attention to people unless they were really worth my time. I frequently started verbal fights in high school if people spoke badly about my friends or family.

I knew a lot of people and there were some that were really close, but most weren't. Everyone respected me, but not everyone wanted to hang out with me. I was very argumentative and stubborn, and socially, I wasn't really popular; but people knew that if they needed something they could ask, and I would try to help if I could.

I had a teacher in 8th grade who told me that I would fail in high school. I made sure to take all honors level classes just to prove her wrong. I excelled in them and earned all As and Bs. That teacher put me in remedial science my freshman year, but I ended up practically teaching that class because the teacher told me that I was too smart to be in there. I helped everyone in that class, including the teacher. Now, I'm thank-

ful for my 8th grade teacherbecause her criticism is what pushed me to excel, even if it was just to prove her wrong.

There was a teacher in middle school who was cheating on her husband. I wanted to write a letter to him so badly, just to call her out, but I didn't. I was going to high school and leaving her behind. Looking back, I'm thankful that I didn't because that wasn't any of my business.

If I could go back, I would definitely be more encouraging and helpful to others. My junior and senior year I was able to be a peer tutor. I really enjoyed helping others get the concept. I was the one giving others my knowledge. That's why I wanted to be a teacher. Even though I would probably understand how to handle it, I hope that I never come across a student like me!

- **Jonathan Loney, 8W9**

One of my earliest memories as a child happened on the playground when I was in 1st grade. There was a boy who had a prosthetic hand that was in the shape of a hook. Other kids were taunting him, calling him "Captain Hook" and other such nonsense. I was livid and immediately stood between him and the group of bullies, spread my arms out to protect him and yelled at them to "LEAVE HIM ALONE!" Looking back, this incident was the first indication of my Type Eight.

I was the middle child of three girls and a model student – hard-working, efficient, never had to be told to do my homework. But I really wanted to fit in. My red hair, freckles, and temper had already begun to set me apart and been a target for bullies who called me 'Red Hot' and let me know often enough that I was the odd one out.

In 4th grade the bullying intensified. I would allow my 'friends' to cheat off my papers; I gave up things that were important to me, like athletics and playing the clarinet, because my 'friends' were mad that I was better than them; I did things that I knew my parents would not approve of. This approval-seeking behavior continued through junior high.

I was always looking for a place to fit in because I felt like I was on the outside 100% of the time. It didn't matter if I was at school, church, clubs, whatever. I hate that I allowed this to happen and wish I could go back and assert my strength.

In high school I retreated deeply into my unhealthy Five space. I secluded myself and withdrew into my head – I really resembled more of a Type Four during that time. I continued to do well in school, but my walls were high and thick. I rebelled in the way that I looked, the people I hung out with, and the activities I did. I struggled with depression and suicidal thoughts. I'm still surprised that none of my teachers seemed to take notice or ask me if I was okay, as my baseline of appearance and behavior had changed drastically over just one summer.

I had one best friend and kept everyone else at arm's length. Then that friend betrayed me in a major way. I was done being vulnerable.

Now that I'm in my 50s I look back and see my Type Eight growing over time into the person I am today – a protector of the vulnerable and a strong independent woman who does big things. I became a high school teacher to put myself in a position to advocate for the 'weak' and those students on the fringe. I adore them. For many of them, like me, their childhood wounds are not coming from home, but from the playground and the classroom. I guess I wanted to help walk them through that, having already been there and survived.

- **Stacy DeVries, 8W9**

Overall, school was a mostly positive experience for me. Elementary school was fun as long as the work was competitive and challenging. I could memorize things very quickly and enjoyed excelling. I also found it easy to make friends. If a teacher was not capable of leading the class or was simply slow and boring, I quickly lost respect and happily took advantage of opportunities to poke fun, pass notes, etc.

At the same time, I began to enjoy putting bullies in their place and squashing the egos of people who thought they were God's gift to the world. I was the instigator in most friend groups and the one perpetually nominated to ask parents or teachers for permission to do things (if it was clear we could just do it and ask forgiveness later, which was preferred if the consequences weren't bad).

High school was when I started to realize I was different from other girls. My friends became more concerned with what others thought, had a harder time standing up for themselves and anguished over boys. I couldn't understand why they couldn't get over things that hurt their feelings. My approach to goals, boys, and school was to simply go after what I wanted and move on if it didn't work out. My friends considered me a voice of reason and always the fun one. In class, I did enough work *to get Bs and a few As so I could go to college but was more interested in life's action (theater, cheerleading, toilet-papering, sleepovers, and more). However, my teachers were often frustrated with me because I didn't take class seriously enough and didn't perform to my potential.*

- **Anne B., 8W7**

ENNEAGRAM TYPE NINE
The Calm & Peaceful Student

*"You may say that I'm a dreamer,
but I'm not the only one.
I hope someday you will join us,
and the world will be as one."*

- *Imagine*, John Lennon

pleasant
caring
accepting
unassertive
complacent
trusting
patient
harmonious

Enneagram Type Nine

Nine students avoid conflict at all costs, but they can find themselves in conflict when they are passive-aggressive, stubborn, emotionally unavailable, complacent, unaware of their feelings and anger, and inattentive to others. This causes conflict with others that they so desperately try to avoid.

Nines desire peace and harmony in the world. They are open, trusting, patient, and kind. At their best, Nines are fully awake to themselves and to life in general. They engage with others and are able to bring people together.

Nine students are able to see all points of view. They are natural peacemakers and mediators, and they are able to bring peace and a sense of tranquility wherever they go. They are calming and free from judgment. They are able to comfort and reassure others.

Nines are the kind of people who always give others the benefit of the doubt because they want to believe the best about everyone. They want to believe that everyone is good. They want every story to have a happy ending. Nines are supreme optimists.

They struggle to believe that their voice, presence, or opinions matter. Because of this, Nines can find themselves trying to be invisible. They can be quiet and keep to themselves, or they can pretend as though everything is great and they don't need anything or any help. They don't want to be a burden to others or cause unnecessary conflict by needing or wanting something.

Nine students can be easily distracted, self-forgetting, and indecisive. Nines merge with every other number on the Enneagram. They do this to avoid tension or conflict. They neglect their own thoughts, ideas, opinions, preferences, needs, wants, etc., to go along with the desires and ideas of others. To Nine students, this seems like the best way to keep the peace.

The Nine sits at the very top of the Enneagram. They have the ability to see all of the different points of view and perspectives. They can see the world from the lens of every other number, and they are able to incorporate the characteristics of each type into their day to day. Because of this, Nines tend to see the world as every other type but their own.

IN A NUTSHELL...

The Nine student is a peacemaker. They want their environment and surroundings to be a pleasant place to be. They are typically relaxed and calm, but every once in a while, you may be able to notice anger or resentment in their tone or expression.

Nines have a hard time making up their mind and can appear to be slower than other children because they have the ability to see things from all angles. It's hard for them to choose or make a decision because they don't know which direction to take.

Core Fear - Tension, conflict, and losing connection with others
Core Desire - Live a peaceful life; free from conflict and tension.
Focus - The wants, needs, preferences, and opinions of others.
Goal - Keep the peace.

Biggest Struggle - Sloth

Nines want to live in a world of peace and harmony. They want to avoid conflict at all costs. They desire to stay in an unrealistic world and avoid negative or hurtful situations. They work really hard to remain unaffected by the anger and negativity of others. The sloth comes into play when Nines 'fall asleep' to their own wants, desires, ideas, abilities, and needs. Nines will merge with others' thoughts, opinions, ideas, desires, wants, and needs in order to keep the peace. This causes them to forget the things that are important to them. They can forget who they are and take on the qualities and characteristics of someone else.

CHARACTERISTICS

Nine students are generally able to be friends with every group. They see the best in others, and they are non-judgmental and accepting. Nines are supportive and generous, and they make wonderful friends. They are wired to see the positive in all people and situations.

Nine students need clear goals and directions. If they are faced with too many choices or too many possibilities, they can feel overwhelmed and shut down. They already have the ability to see many different points of view; having too many options can become paralyzing.

Nines love to be acknowledged and praised for their successes and achievements, but they may also get shy and embarrassed when they receive them. Keep praising them and applauding them. They feel that their presence doesn't matter, so anytime you can assure them that they do matter, do it.

When they feel overwhelmed or find themselves in conflict, they tend to take a step back and find something comforting to do. They will avoid reality and stay in a comfortable place doing a familiar and routine activity. Nine students always want to be comfortable, in all areas of life. They enjoy staying in their comfort zone and feel no reason to test the boundaries.

Nine students have a hard time making decisions. They feel that their decision may not be what others would choose, so instead of causing potential tension or conflict, they will let someone else make a decision for them. Nines will go with the flow to keep the peace.

COMMUNICATION STYLE

Nines students have a very pleasant tone of voice. They are calm, relaxed, and peaceful. They are social and can get along with everyone. For the most part, your Nine students will follow the rules and talk with their peers when it's appropriate to do so. Remember, they want to avoid conflict and tension.

Nines aren't going to compete in a conversation. If they have something to say, but never get the opportunity to say it, they won't say it at all. In a conversation with a Nine student, make sure you give them space to chime in. That way if they do have something to say, they are being given a clear opportunity to contribute.

Below are a few suggestions on how to effectively communicate with a Calm and Peaceful Student:

- Most of the time, they are genuinely okay to go with the flow, but Nines don't like to be told what do to.
- Nines can take their time when telling a story or sharing their thoughts. Be patient, and don't interrupt them.
- Nines need time to think and process. Give them time to digest the question or situation and the different points of view before expecting a response.
- Reassure them that their ideas and opinions are valued.
- Nines won't fight for attention or fight to be heard. If someone talks over them, they will give up and stop talking.

LEARNING STYLE

Nine students love routine. They love structure. They love knowing what to expect. They appreciate repetition. The more they see or hear something, the more likely they are to retain it.

Nines enjoy physical movement in class. Incorporating movement breaks or classroom exercises into the lesson would help keep the Nine students engaged. When they are able to get their whole self-involved in the learning process, they are going to process the information better.

Nines need clear expectations, goals, and directions. They can get easily distracted and tend to procrastinate, so if large projects can be broken down into smaller pieces, the project as a whole will be less overwhelming. They also prefer to have all of the information upfront so they can process everything before diving in. Nine students would enjoy getting reading material the day before a class discussion.

WORK ETHIC

Nine students get the work done by the time it is due. They may procrastinate for weeks on a project and get the whole thing finished in a few days, but they work hard when they need to. Students who lean into their One wing may be better at organizing and managing their time to make sure projects get completed before the last minute. Nine students also enjoy frequent breaks.

Nines, like Twos, are concerned with the needs of those around them. They may worry that someone else doesn't understand the directions before they will notice or be concerned that they don't understand themselves. They don't want to bother their teachers, so they are more likely to ask a peer for help before ever considering asking you. The 1, 2, 3 Rule may help a Nine student feel comfortable asking their teacher a question. Ask 1 friend, ask 2 friends, ask 3 friends, then ask the teacher. If three other classmates don't have the answer, then it is encouraged to ask the teacher for help. This allows you to meet them where they are. They don't want to bother you, but you are giving them permission, after doing what they would naturally do anyway.

High-energy classrooms can be draining for a Nine (and a Five). While a Seven would love to have a high-energy classroom all day, every day, that would be a Nine student's worst nightmare. This is where balance comes in. I know it's not possible to please everyone, all the time, at the same time, but it is possible to rotate strategies, so you are benefitting every student.

Report card feedback may say: Student is pleasant and friendly towards others, student would benefit by managing their time more effectively, or student is able to cooperate and partner up with anyone in the class.

PREFERRED CLASSROOM ENVIRONMENT

Nine students need a low stress and no conflict environment. They prefer a stable environment where they know and understand the routine. Nines seek comfort in all things. If there are more casual spaces set up in the classroom, Nines will typically gravitate towards them, if they have a choice.

Nine students are able to see the big picture and different points of view. They are able to bring unlikely things or people together and can play devil's advocate in order to help mediate conflict between peers. Overall, if Nine students are in a happy and comfortable environment, they will feel at peace.

WINGS

The wings attached to Type Nine are The Opinionated and Confident Student (Type Eight) and The Serious and Hard-Working Student (Type One). These wings can be abbreviated as 9W8 and 9W1.

THE 9W8

The Type Nine with the Eight wing is more sociable, engaging, encouraging, and independent. They are more assertive and expressive. They seek and enjoy comfort. When struggling, they are more likely to have a powerful temper if they are pushed too far, overlooked, or disrespected. This wing is inspiring because they are gentle, but powerful. They assert themselves on the behalf of others and they make sure everyone is valued and seen.

THE 9W1

The Type Nine with the One wing is more idealistic, principled, and cerebral. They want to do what is right by everyone and they care about fairness and equality. When struggling, they become quieter and more withdrawn. They can be more judgmental and critical. This wing is inspiring because they are great mediators. The Nine is able to see all perspectives and the One insists on truth and objectivity.

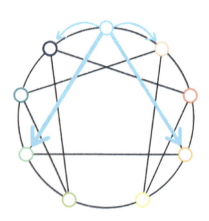

THINGS TO LEARN

Nine students frequently don't know where to start. It would help them to narrow their focus and zone in on what is really important. Narrowing their focus will also help them with prioritizing and concentrating on one specific thing. Nines would also benefit from knowing that they are in a safe place to express their feelings. They need reassurance that they are seen and heard, and that they matter.

IN STRESS

In stress, a Nine moves to an average to an unhealthy Type Six. They can become overly worried and anxious, which can cause them to focus on worst-case scenarios. Their minds may be restless, and they can become irritable and easily frustrated. They realize that they have put things off for too long and will frantically try to make up for lost time. They may become reactive and defensive. You may catch them worrying or stressing about the possibility that they have forgotten something important.

IN GROWTH

In growth, a Nine moves to a healthy Type Three. They develop a go-getter attitude, and they get things done. They are able to show up for their own lives and assert themselves as well as their opinions and preferences. They recognize that their presence is a gift to others. Nines in growth will take the time to discover what they are passionate about. They grow increasingly more confident. They quit procrastinating. They make a plan, stick to it, and accomplish their goals. They are able to speak up and share their knowledge and insights.

LEVELS OF DEVELOPMENT

Healthy levels:

Level 1 - (at their best) They are fully connected to themselves and others. They are completely fulfilled. They are at peace with themselves and are able to form profound relationships with others.
Level 2 - They are extremely accepting and receptive. They are emotionally stable, and they are not self-conscious. They trust themselves and others. They are at ease with life. They are patient, good-natured, and genuine.
Level 3 - They are optimistic and supportive. They have a calming influence, and they are able to bring people together. They are good mediators and communicators.

Average levels:

Level 4 - They fear confrontations and become accommodating to avoid conflicts. They go along with others and say 'yes' to things they don't really want to do. They fall into expectations and roles.
Level 5 - They are active, but inattentive and disengaged with others. They can be complacent and walk away from problems and sweep them under the rug rather than face them head on. They tune out reality and are unwilling to focus on conflicts. They are indifferent.
Level 6 - They minimize problems to maintain peace. They are stubborn and believe that a situation won't change. Peers become frustrated by their lack of response and procrastination.

Unhealthy levels:

Level 7 - They become neglectful, which can be dangerous for others. They are ineffective and dissociate themselves from conflicts and confrontations. They believe that they aren't capable of facing their problems.
Level 8 - They tune out anything that could negatively affect them. They become numb and get to the point where they eventually can't function.
Level 9 - They are so disoriented that they eventually abandon themselves. It's possible that they develop multiple personalities.

DEFENSE MECHANISM

The defense mechanism for the Nine is narcotization or dissociation. Nines use narcotization or dissociation to avoid conflict and to maintain a self-image of being peaceful. Narcotization or dissociation is using familiar routines or comforts to "fall asleep to oneself." If something feels too big, too difficult, or too much to handle, Nines will take a walk, watch their favorite show, read their favorite book, or find another comfortable activity so they can numb out or check out from the real world. If these comfort seeking activities are disrupted, the Nine may become agitated. This conflict avoidance with others prevents them from being fully present and engaging in relationships. When they avoid their own internal conflicts, they begin to merge with others and forget who they are.

CHILDHOOD PATTERNS

Nine children are connected (or desire to be) equally to both parental figures, or any other authority figure who resembles a parent. Because of their natural empathy, they tend to bear most of the emotional weight of their entire family. They consciously and unconsciously merge with their parents on what is expected. Nines take on their parents' expectations as their own. They become overwhelmed with trying to please both parents and other authority figures. Nines know what both parents wish and desire, so they do what they can to keep the peace and make sure both parents are happy. When they become overwhelmed, they find solitude in their imagination where they have freedom and peace. If they are in a home full of conflict, they may physically retreat somewhere free from tension.

Nines learn how to keep a low profile at home by not asserting themselves or asking for too much. They feel that this will keep their home peaceful and free from tension. They feel that they need to be invisible, so their presence and their needs will not create or add any more conflict. Nines think that not being seen will bring them peace.

What actually happens is, they become invisible and unnoticed by others. By doing this, they also lose touch with themselves and the things that make them special: their desires, needs, opinions, passions, and values.

TRIGGERS FOR CONFLICT

When Nines are triggered, they will withdraw. They may not say anything and will hide how they are truly feeling. They don't want to create space for more conflict. They may show a little bit of tension in their facial expression but remain unaware of their anger. They may take their anger and frustration out on someone else who wasn't even involved in the original source of tension or conflict.

Conflict in Nines may be triggered by any sort of disruption to their peace or harmony. They don't want to be taken advantage of or told what to do. Conflict may arise if they feel disrespected or overlooked. They are likely to feel triggered if someone directly confronts them about something or when they see someone being rude, insensitive, mean, or disrespectful to others.

A HOW-TO GUIDE FOR THE CALM AND PEACEFUL STUDENT

- To help them develop their confidence, show interest in their opinions and ask for their input.
- Create opportunities for a Nine student to say what's on their mind. You may have to model this for them until they are comfortable enough to speak their mind.
- Even though they may not give their opinion, remember to ask for their input so they feel that their opinion matters.
- It's important to pay attention to their level of development:
  - A healthy Type Nine is accepting of others and completely at peace with themselves.
  - An average Type Nine is accommodating and conflict avoidant. They minimize problems to keep the peace.
  - An unhealthy Type Nine tunes out anything negative and begins to numb themselves to the world around them.
- If a student is at a healthy level, encourage and reassure them that they are on the right path
- If a student is at an unhealthy level, pay attention to their environment. What may be triggering their negative behaviors and attitudes? Find ways to work with their strengths and make them more confident.
- Pushing, nagging, or focusing on their mistakes and flaws will more than likely only make matters worse. If needed, seek professional help and guidance.

FAMOUS ENNEAGRAM NINES

- Ronald Reagan
- Zooey Deschanel
- Walt Disney
- Alicia Keys
- Barack Obama
- Morgan Freeman
- Queen Elizabeth II
- Dorothy (*The Wizard of Oz*)

TYPE NINE QUESTIONNAIRE

Does the student:

☐ avoid conflict at all costs?

☐ go with the flow?

☐ procrastinate?

☐ seem to be more comfortable if they are close to you?

☐ tend to get distracted easily?

☐ find it difficult to make a decision?

☐ enjoy comforting activities like watching tv, reading a book, playing on the computer, or taking a walk?

☐ regularly accommodate others?

☐ blend in with the crowd?

☐ seem to be easy-going?

ADULT REFLECTIONS ON BEING A CALM AND PEACEFUL STUDENT

1. I remember telling my friends that my goal for school was to stay under the teacher's radar. I didn't want to be a star student and I didn't want to flunk out.
2. I avoided drama and cliques like the plague. I stayed involved in a lot of different sports and music, and I always kept good grades.
3. I went to smaller private school. I had a really nice group of friends and I got along with teachers for the most part. I did my best to stay out of trouble.
4. I floated around and could fit in with every group. I was voted most friendly and best personality.
5. I was pretty shy. I was never in the popular crowd, but I had my own little tribe.
6. I was an average student who could have been extraordinary, but instead chose to be extra ordinary to blend in.
7. I had a pretty small group of friends that constantly changed as events changed. For example, if my friend got a boyfriend, I would have become the third wheel so I removed myself from that relationship so they wouldn't have to remove me.
8. I wanted to work hard but I didn't feel like I had any direction since my mom had a 9th grade education. School wasn't important to me. It wasn't until college that I made the decision to succeed.
9. I was friends with everyone, and I stayed out of the regular high school drama. I never said a negative word about anyone. Gossip wasn't my thing.
10. I struggled (and still do) with figuring out what was the most important thing on my list. To me, everything was important, but I didn't know how to prioritize and so I ended up waiting until the last minute to do anything. I was/am a huge procrastinator.

WHAT BEING A CALM AND PEACEFUL STUDENT WAS LIKE:

In 4th grade a new boy asked me out. Because I was in 4th grade, I didn't know what that meant so I said no. Well, he punched me in the face and then I punched him back in the face. For a few months after that, he kept telling me that he was going to kill me. He finally got kicked out of school, thankfully, but I think that's when I started to try to be more invisible and conflict-avoidant. I literally felt like conflict could lead to death.

I have two older sisters, they are 6 and 8 years older than me. My oldest sister and I basically pretended like we didn't need anything because my middle sister just required so much attention from my parents. She was constantly in screaming matches with my mom and was always causing conflict. I just tried to keep the peace as much as possible.

We moved from New York to New Jersey in middle school. I went from having a ton of friends and playing a lot of sports to not knowing anyone and being the weird, new kid. I ended up trying out for basketball and then was encouraged to try field hockey, too. That really helped me to make new friends.

We moved to a really snobby place. There was definitely the mean girls group. I hated it. I felt like I didn't matter at school, and I didn't matter at home. My older sisters were in college by the time we moved, so they were gone. When I got home, no one was there because my parents had to work.

The high school I went to had a few middle schools that fed into the one high school. That was nice because everyone had to figure out their place. Everyone had a fresh start. I always did well in school. I wanted to do well. I put the pressure on myself to do well because I wanted to please my parents and my teachers. I felt like if I did well, then they would be happy, and I would feel important and like I mattered.

In 9th grade I played basketball and I had an issue with the coach. Because of that issue, I ended up quitting basketball, which I regret to this day. Basketball was my thing and all of the sudden I didn't do it anymore.

I found a book called "Eat to Win." I picked it up to help me get better at sports, but ultimately, I got out of control with it and ended up in the hospital. I developed anorexia because I was good at controlling what went into my body. I didn't have basketball anymore; I didn't have anything that I was good at anymore. I was good at controlling my food intake. I lost a lot of weight. Again, I felt like my presence didn't matter. I kept thinking "well, what if I just don't exist?"

I was pretty organized, too. Everything had to be in order. Food, loading the dishwasher a certain way, school; and it's funny because I'm not this organized now, I wish I could get some of that back.

- **female, 9W1**

In middle school I was conservative and not easily influenced. I was definitely a people-pleaser, though. I was on top of my school assignments and made sure I got good grades. I had a few best friends but many other casual friendships, the kind where you say "hey" in the hallway.

I struggled at home. My parents (mom and stepdad) took in foster kids, so eventually I began to feel left out. I didn't feel important to them anymore. I couldn't do extracurricular activities because I didn't have a ride. The only thing I was able to participate in was band because it was right after school, and someone was able to take me home. I resented my homelife a lot and I kept it all to myself. I got to see my real dad every other weekend and it was fine, but he never really engaged with me, so I was always on my own.

In high school, things went downhill. I wanted someone to notice me and love me so badly that I did whatever I needed to do to feel that. I realized that I could get the attention that I wanted and needed from high school boys, so I did. I was very promiscuous. My schoolwork suffered and my people-pleasing tendencies increased. I would literally do anything for someone to pay attention to me. I barely graduated high school and I often got in trouble for skipping class.

Life at home was distant and cold. No one engaged with me, and I didn't engage with them. I became an outcast and I hated who I was. I was so incredibly lost.

- **Tiffany Spencer, 9W8**

I was an overachiever in school. I leaned hard into my growth path and my One wing. I was in every club. I won every scholarship. I got really good grades. My dad passed away when I was 14 and that was a very traumatic time for me. I would like to believe that I coped well, but looking back, I think my overpacked schedule was my way of avoiding having to deal with reality.

Socially, I got along with everyone. I grew up in a small rural town (graduating class had 89 students). I could hang out with any group. I lettered in sports in high school. I was in musicals and the choir. I was in the gifted program and chess club. I rebuilt a Jeep in auto shop. I won a drafting competition. And, on top of all of those things, I worked after school for a farmer.

Though I was not the leader or most popular in any group, I did it all. Looking back now, maybe it was my Nine merging in every direction. I made friends with everyone even though they didn't run in the same crowd together. I continued those high school relationships through college and beyond. My best friends now are those same people from high school.

- **male, 9W1**

Putting It All Together

My first year teaching I had a student who I wanted to take home and adopt as my own. His home life was terrible. His school life was rough. His behavior and attitude were dismal. To keep his privacy, let's call him Austin.

I began my teaching career in January 2011. I started on the first day of the second semester. The other teachers I worked with were so incredibly helpful and kind. They knew it was my first day ever in a classroom. We all knew that I had no idea what I was doing, but it was okay. The kids didn't know, and I got through my first day without any problems.

Because I started mid-year, my colleagues already knew the kids on my rosters. They were telling me who the amazing kids were and who to watch out for. Austin was first on the 'who to watch out for' list. Not a single teacher liked him or enjoyed having him in their class, if I am remembering correctly, and that broke my heart.

Austin was a 7th grade boy and I'm sure he was well aware of the fact that none of his teachers liked him. This was many years before I had even heard of the Enneagram - but I still feel like this is an important story to share.

By June 2011, Austin improved his grades and work ethic. It may have only been in my class, but he worked. He stayed after school with me for tutoring. He tried. He cared.

He fell asleep during his end of year testing. He got the lowest score possible, because he didn't finish the test. Time ran out. Students who were close to passing were given a single opportunity to retake the test. Students who scored where Austin scored, didn't get another chance.

I spoke to my principal at the time and begged for Austin to get another chance.

You see, Austin fell asleep because he had slept in a car the night before. Not the ideal situation for anyone, for any regular day of school, but certainly not for the night before a big exam. And it wasn't his fault; I'm quite certain he didn't want to sleep in a car. Austin had worked really, really hard to master those skills. He needed a fair chance. He wanted another opportunity.

Fortunately, my principal agreed, and Austin was given another chance. Austin had not ever passed a single end of year exam. He failed them all, miserably. He never cared. But on this one, his final score was one point away from passing. He didn't pass, but he lit up with excitement. Austin was so proud, and I was proud of him too.

Looking back, I don't know what Enneagram type he was, but I am a Type Four. I can point out many times in my life where others have warned me about someone or couldn't understand why I thought a certain person was incredible. I guess I've just always made those decisions for myself, and I try to see the best in everyone. It's my job to figure out a person's character; no one else gets to decide that for me.

But there are a few people I can think of who I really, really respect and like, that many others don't. And to be fair and honest, there are also a few people who I do not like at all, and I can't really give a clear reason why other than, I just don't trust them and I get a bad vibe.

But overall, Fours really want to belong, they know and understand that longing, and they want it for others who are out there being authentically themselves and not being accepted for it. It's beautiful.

Every type is beautiful, every type has amazing things to offer, and every type has flaws.

The point of Austin's story, and my input at the end of his story, is to share that it really doesn't matter what others think.

Teachers, I urge you to please stop talking to each other about your students. I'll be the first to admit that my hands are not clean. After a few years into my teaching career, I fell into the trap. I warned teachers about their incoming students. I'm guilty. I own it.

You see, I thought that I was being helpful. Teachers believe that they are being helpful by sharing who is great and who isn't. But honestly, that just takes away that student's opportunity to have a fresh start and that teacher's opportunity to form his or her own opinions.

Cue the Enneagram. Insert knowledge. Remove judgment.

I understand that this can feel like a lot. Teachers are overworked as it is. I understand that asking you to learn the Enneagram is adding something else to your already overflowing cup. But trust me on this: when you understand who you are, and you understand the Enneagram completely, your classroom will change.

So often we find ourselves in parent-teacher conferences discussing how the student can improve, and what they can do to engage, behave, and just be better. A room full of adults telling the parent all of the ways the student is falling short. But what if we, the teachers and parents, are the ones falling short?

I challenge you to flip the script. It's not the student who needs to change. It's the adults around them. Their teachers, their parents.

As adults, we have more power over the children in our lives with our mindset and our behaviors. Our words don't mean much, but our actions speak volumes. Our outlook and our demeanor can shift an entire room.

"As children develop, their brains 'mirror' their parent's brain. In other words, the parent's own growth and development, or lack of those, impact the child's brain. As parents become more aware and emotionally healthy, their children reap the rewards and move toward health as well. That means that integrating and cultivating your own brain is one of the most loving and generous gifts you can give to your children."

- Daniel J. Siegel, MD

The word parent in that quote refers to a parent, teacher, or any caregiver; anyone who has a significant role in a child's life.

This change isn't going to happen overnight. It's a gradual process, but change will come. Change begins with us, and trickles down from there.

I spoke with an Enneagram coach who also works with parents, students, and teachers. She had a child who demonstrated Type Eight tendencies. He was thirteen and he was a bully. He demonstrated his power and control at school in a lot of negative ways. He was challenging and was constantly being disciplined. But the reality of the situation was, he was completely powerless at home. He didn't have any control and he was being dominated. All he wanted was to have control over his own life.

After learning about his life at home, she coached him and worked with his teacher to cultivate a plan to give his leadership qualities an opportunity to grow. Step by step, they created an opportunity, and this child was put in charge of a group of elementary aged children who were getting picked on. These kids were getting their lunches stolen and their toys were getting taken. He was placed in a role to have positive power and he ran with it.

Those children adored him. He was their protector. He took care of them. He made sure they were safe. He turned into a real hero, a real leader.

From then on, the bullying tactics from this child stopped. He was finally in a position of power, and he used it positively. He had control. He no longer needed to search for it in negative ways.

The Enneagram is life changing. Using it in the classroom and at home can shift your entire universe, if you let it. Ultimately, the choice is yours. The children in your world are our future. Don't we want to raise strong, confident, and emotionally-intelligent human beings?

Don't we want classrooms full of students who feel seen, who feel heard, who feel understood, who feel valued? Wouldn't that change the dynamics? Wouldn't that change their whole trajectory? Wouldn't that ultimately change the world?

"Your emotional awareness and ability to handle feelings will determine your success and happiness in life."

- John Gottman, PhD

Every child deserves a chance. Unfortunately, not every child has the same opportunity to have one based on their environment outside of school. Every child has an opportunity, but as you know, some have many, many more obstacles to overcome.

Teachers, you matter. I know you know that, but I also know that some days it's difficult to remember. Some days, you feel like you just aren't getting through to anyone. Use of the Enneagram won't make your classrooms perfect, but they will be more manageable, more loving, more supportive, and more compassionate.

For the most part, students are with their teachers more often than they are with their own parents. Be the change that they need.

The Enneagram is a game changer, if you allow it to be. It can transform lives and communication with others. It can depersonalize triggering behaviors. It can increase your amount of empathy and your understanding and compassion for others.

In the classroom, it can completely change the dynamics. Have you ever wondered why you gravitate to some students so easily and find others to be such a challenge? Only to discover that those challenging students are actually wonderful for other teachers. I'm sure you probably brushed it off as a difference in personalities, which is correct. But the students aren't the ones who need to change, the adults are.

Change begins with you and trickles down from there. So, tell me, how do you want to make an impact?

A better you *is* a better them.

Acknowledgements

First and foremost, I want to thank God. I never wanted to be a teacher. Okay, maybe for a minute in high school because my math teacher was so incredible, and I wanted to be just like her. (Thanks, Mrs. Liz Brown! PS. I still remember the quadratic equation formula song!) But aside from those few weeks in high school, teaching wasn't on my career choice list. Not even at the bottom.

I wanted to be a journalist. Or an obstetrician, but chemistry and I didn't get along too well, so that threw the idea of med school and nursing school out of the window.

I graduated from East Carolina University in 2010 with a communications degree. My college education put me in a convenient spot where teaching was an option because my degree was relevant to the English/Language Arts subject. I had to go back to college to take a few education courses, but that happened after I had already been hired.

You guys, God knew what He was doing back in 2010, and He knew what was coming. He knew what I needed to be doing. He knew I needed classroom experience in order to move forward.

I never would have been able to write this book if I hadn't spent 10.5 years in the classroom. And for that, I am forever grateful.

Thank you to Terry McGinnis, Stephanie Holleman, and Diane Childress. I had many administrators throughout my time in the classroom, but those three were second to none. I wouldn't be here without my first admin team (Terry and Stephanie). They believed in me and encouraged me to start the lateral entry process to become a full time teacher. Diane was my last principal and is a model for what true leadership looks like. I was blessed to have taught under her leadership for three years.

I would also like to thank my family: my husband, my children, my parents, my sister. You are my inspiration day in and day out. I wouldn't be who I am today without any of you. I love you all so, so much. Thank you for believing in me. Thank you for supporting me.

Thank you to all of the amazing Enneagram scholars and teachers who have come before me. Thank you to Ian Morgan Cron and Suzanne Stabile for writing The Road Back to You. That book is one of my absolute favorites and it really deepened my Enneagram knowledge. Thank you, Beth McCord, for creating a Christian based Enneagram certification program. I am forever thankful that my training is rooted in the gospel.

About The Author

Sarah Dutton Waxman is a wife and a mother of two boys. She taught in a middle school classroom for over a decade teaching both math and English Language Arts to 6th, 7th, and 8th grade students. She resigned from education in 2021 to pursue her work with the Enneagram. She is a certified Enneagram Coach through Beth McCord's program *Become an Enneagram Coach*.

Sarah is a former educator turned coach. She is an author and a public speaker. She conducts workshops and trainings for parents and educators, both in-person and virtually. She travels to schools across the US, and her signature program, *That's A Big Idea*, provides schools and districts hands-on support over an entire school year. Sarah also works one-on-one and in a group capacity with parents and educators to help them discover and dive deep into their Enneagram type. Once they discover who they truly are, the conversation changes to help them better understand their own children and the students in their classrooms.

You can find Sarah on Instagram and TikTok at @sarahwaxmanofficial, check her out online at www.sarahwaxman.coach, and tune in to her podcast: Raising EnneaKids.

REFERENCES

Biffi, Megan. "The Enneagram in Learning and Development." Integrative 9, 11 Apr. 2019, www.integrative9.com/media/articles/27/The-Ennea-gram-in-Learning and-Development.

Cron, Ian Morgan. *The Road Back to You: An Enneagram Journey to Self-discovery*. Downers Grove: InterVarsity, 2016. Print.

Fitzel, Rob. "The Nine Types of Students." The Enneagram, www.fitzel.ca/enneagram/students.html.

Hall, Stephanie Barron. "Communication Styles by Enneagram Type." Nine Types Co., 1 May 2020, ninetypes.co/blog/communication-styles by-enneagram-type.

Lapid-Bogda, Ginger. *Bringing out the Best in Yourself at Work: How to Use the ENNEAGRAM System for Success*. New York: McGraw Hill, 2004.

McCord, Beth. *Become An Enneagram Coach*. Your Enneagram Coach. https://www.yourenneagramcoach.com/bec

O'Hanrahan, Peter. "The Enneagram Defense System." The Enneagram At Work, https://theenneagramatwork.com/defense systems

Palmer, Helen. *The Enneagram in Love & Work: Understanding Your Intimate & Business Relationships*. New York: HarperOne, 1995. Print.

Riso, Don Richard, and Russ Hudson. *Discovering Your Personality Type*. New York: Houghton Mifflin, 2003. Print.

Still, Jane. "Enneagram Personalities of Students." Compassionate Learn-ing, 10 Sept. 2016, compassionatelearning.org/enneagram personali-ties-students-copingstrategies-emotionalintelligence compassion/.

Vancil, Marilyn. *Self to Lose Self to Find: A Biblical Approach to the 9 Enneagram Types*. Convergent Books, 2020. Print.

Wagele, Elizabeth. *The Enneagram of Parenting: The 9 Types of Children and How to Raise Them Successfully*. New York: HarperOne, 2010. Print.

Made in the USA
Las Vegas, NV
06 September 2022